Children Starting School

Children Starting School

A GUIDE TO SUCCESSFUL TRANSITIONS AND
TRANSFERS FOR TEACHERS AND ASSISTANTS

HILARY FABIAN

David Fulton Publishers
London

David Fulton Publishers Ltd
Ormond House, 26–27 Boswell Street, London WC1N 3JZ

First Published in Great Britain in 2002 by David Fulton Publishers

British Cataloguing in Publication Data
A catalogue record for this book is available from the British Library.

ISBN 1 85346 807 X

Typeset by Mark Heslington, Scarborough, North Yorkshire
Printed and bound in Great Britain by Bell & Bain Ltd., Glasgow.

Contents

Preface

The education of young children is a current political priority. If it is to work well then teachers and other practitioners need to ensure that the start of education outside the home is a positive milestone in lifelong learning. In addition to starting school, children make transitions through school and transfers between schools. There is an increasing emphasis on the social inclusion of minority groups such as travellers. These, and other mobile populations, such as children of armed forces personnel, can make frequent transfers between schools which can affect their learning. In the light of this, the induction to school and subsequent transitions that children make need to be understood to help make the transfer between settings smooth and untroubled for children and their parents.

My interest in induction and transitions stems from my own moves between teaching posts and my work with several Reception classes over a number of years in England and Germany. There are similarities between staff induction to a new place of work and children's induction to school, and it is evident that the quality of this settling-in period is important in enabling continuing development. In this book I draw on research, theory and practice to present ways in which practitioners, working with parents, can support the start of school both collectively and individually. It is underpinned by principles about the way in which social and emotional well-being support children's learning and is grounded in the practical needs of pupils, parents and practitioners. The book is based on research from my PhD and includes case study material drawn from 50 children and their parents at the start of school. I am deeply indebted to the children, parents and staff who took part in that study and who gave so much of themselves, their time and their thoughts. Without them, many of the case studies in the book would not have been possible as the 'conversations' in them are created by drawing material from their interviews and comprise a 'meshing of individual narratives into new collectives and individual wholes' (Gura 1996: 43). My sincere thanks go to Professor Christine Pascal and Professor Philip Gammage who gave me guidance, advice and encouragement throughout the writing of my PhD and this book.

Activities in the book developed from an early years Continuing Professional Development module on induction and transitions which I taught at the Manchester Metropolitan University between 1998 and 2000. My thanks go to those students who undertook the module and who wanted a book that addressed issues about starting school. I am also grateful for the support and encouragement of numerous friends and colleagues. A special thank you to my husband, Mike Carter, who listened to me rehearse my ideas, challenged my thinking and read through various drafts of the book.

Before going any further, I would like to clarify some of the words used in the book. The term *preschool* will be used for the range of services offering education and care to children below statutory school age. It is based on the definition of early childhood education and care adopted by the Organisation for Economic Cooperation and Development (OECD) countries involved in the Thematic Review of Early Childhood Education and Care Policy project. It refers to the full range of care and education provision including 'organised home-based, centre-based and school-based arrangements for children below compulsory school age, regardless of administrative auspices, funding sources, staffing, or programme emphasis' (Neuman 2000: 1).

The term *parents* can no longer be based on the assumption that children live with two adults who are their natural parents, although this is still the case for many. There have been massive changes in the nature of family life, thus Bastiani and Doyle (1994) suggest that there are now:

> children in lone parent families; children who live in 'reconstituted' families, with a mixture of natural and step-parents; children who are 'looked after' by local authorities; and children who live in families where cultural arrangements for parenting are shaped by significant differences of language and religion. (Bastiani and Doyle 1994: 20)

Therefore, when the word 'parent(s)' is used it refers to those adults who are, or act as, the parent(s) of the child.

Burke (1987: viii) states that 'the most common perception of induction is that it occurs as one enters a new position . . . This narrow view ignores many early and important steps preceding the entrance to a first position . . .'.

For the purposes of this book the word *induction* comprises the introduction to school from the first visit to the time at which the child settles. It constitutes all the activities and experiences that children may meet and includes 'all the conditions and processes by which individuals gain direction and encouragement through increased understanding' (Burke 1987: ix).

Transition describes the moves that pupils experience within a school and include:

- the time between the first visit and settling in;

- a change such as a long-term physical move from one classroom to another during, or at the end of, a school year;
- a change of teacher during, or at the end of, a school year;
- a change of children such as a group of children moving into, or out of, the class either during, or at the end of, a school year.

Transfer refers to the move from one school to another or one phase to another, once full-time, statutory education has begun.

The purpose of the book is to assist teachers and practitioners in developing the best practice when working with new children (and their families) as they start school, change classes or transfer between schools. It draws on identified good practice but it is not a tool kit, as the contexts for starting school vary. Rather, the book offers principles, strategies and procedures for consideration when deciding on ways to manage the induction to school and to develop partnerships that will reduce discontinuities and promote seamless learning during transitions.

Hilary Fabian
September 2001

CHAPTER 1

Introduction

> Children, like adults, enjoy and are stimulated by novelty and change. The first day of school, the transfer to 'big school', are landmarks in the process of growing up. Even when children are apprehensive, they look forward to change . . . But if change is to stimulate and not to dishearten, it must be carefully prepared and not too sudden. (DES 1967, para. 427)

The start of school is recognised as a major transition in a child's life but it is not a standardised process with a prescribed set of practices to be followed, as there is a wide range of contextual and socio-cultural variability. Children approach school with a diversity of individual experiences, attitudes, expectations and developmental differences. Children at this stage are facing developmental challenges as well as having to adapt to a new environment, routine and people. The start of school also has an impact on parents and family life. Early years practitioners planning transition programmes for new children who are commencing school need to be aware of factors that influence children's early adjustment to school and ways in which they can make a stress-free bridge from preschool to school. Although this may not be the first transition for many children, its importance is acknowledged as being a critical factor, in determining not only children's success at school but also their response to future transitions (Rutter and Rutter 1992). It is important, therefore, that the start of school is a healthy life-transition, based on best practice. To get it right requires an understanding of the complexity and diversity of the start of preschool and school, and knowledge about ways in which the transition can be supported. The process is about having structures ready for children as well as giving children the tools to cope with change.

The importance of achieving an untroubled and successful start to school is essential because of the long-term benefits this has on future learning. A study by Tizard *et al.* (1988) found that initial success during the Reception class led to a virtuous cycle whereby those pupils who made the greatest progress remained high achievers throughout their primary schooling. Not only is a smooth start seen as being influential in helping children to learn, but also, because childhood is regarded as having the potential antecedent for adult neurosis (James and Prout 1997), each new start becomes important for the future. The first impressions that children have of school may affect subsequent attitudes as 'memories remain with us and may still affect our behaviour many years later' (Pascal 1990: 1).

Starting school is taking place at an increasingly younger age. The compulsory school starting age in England, introduced in the 1944 Education Act, is the term after a child's fifth birthday. However, this is, in effect, being reduced through a number of government education initiatives. The Nursery Education Voucher Scheme that was introduced nationally in April 1997 and ended on 31 August 1997 (DfEE 1997a) brought early entry to school for many children. The introduction of the Nursery Education Grant and Early Years Development Plans (DfEE 1997b) continued the emphasis on nursery education. Since September 1998 there is a nursery place for all four-year-olds whose parents want it, many of which are in the Reception class of a school. Furthermore, places are now being offered to three-year-olds in some schools. Coupled with this is the socio-political context that has brought about changes in family and work structures, creating further pressure for early admission. These frequent initiatives have led parents to scrutinise the effects on their children's transition to full-time education (Campbell 2000) and have raised a growing awareness among educators of the need to attend to transitional entitlements (Lawrence 1994: 162). The integration, coordination and collaboration of childcare and education is also leading authorities to re-evaluate their organisational model for the care and education of young children in an attempt to meet the needs of parents and children (Osgood and Sharp 2000).

The 1988 Education Reform Act brought greater emphasis on partnership between schools and parents, and on parental choice of school (DES 1991; DFE 1994). Formula funding under the Local Management of Schools directly links school income to pupil numbers and has led to marketing to attract customers (Tomlinson 1993; Foskett 1998). This, in turn, encourages schools to compete for pupils.

Policy changes to raise standards have led to the introduction of Early Learning Goals for three- to five-year-olds (QCA 2000); the introduction, under section 9 of the Education (Schools) Act 1992, of inspection of schools (Ofsted 1995); and the introduction of inspection of publicly funded nursery education under section 5 of the Nursery Education and Grant Maintained Schools Act 1996 (Ofsted 1998). There is a high expectation on pupils to succeed. The introduction of an accredited baseline assessment scheme in September 1998 for all maintained schools (SCAA 1997), to help teachers plan and check rates of pupil progress, added to this expectation. As a result of these initiatives and the emphasis on performance, starting school makes 'a range of potentially stressful demands' (Ghaye and Pascal 1988: 3) on practitioners, pupils and their parents.

Managing change

Change is welcomed by many and does not necessarily cause any problems, but school entry and transfer can pose major difficulties for some children. The change from home and preschool to school involves coping with physical, social and philosophical differences. Marked discontinuities between home and school can impede learning (Cleave *et al.* 1982). Factors such as speaking a language other than English at home, being a boy and being young can also disadvantage some children at the start of school (Margetts 2000). Hughes *et al.* (1979), in their research into the process of adjustment to school, found that 13 per cent of children were found to be having difficulties coping with school after half a term and suggest that some kind of emotional disturbance was involved, although for the majority the difficulties of starting school were relatively short-lived. Children must make sense of the differences between home and school, and overcome any obstacles if they are to succeed. Managing the induction programme and supporting children through discontinuities is the central theme of this book.

Physical discontinuities
One of the most significant influences on learning is the setting in which it occurs. Our physical surroundings have an impact on the way we behave because every aspect of our surroundings sends out subtle psychological messages (McGavin 2001). The style of decoration, the lighting and the physical aspects, such as the furniture, affect performance. The physical conditions in which children work are often translated into their attitudes to learning. Some children face substantial changes in their physical environment at the start of school. These include the condition and size of the building, the amount of classroom resources and equipment, the location of facilities such as the cloakroom and toilets, and the availability of outdoor areas. Cleave *et al.* (1982: 39) identified three features of the environment that are critical at this time: 'the *scale* of the child's setting, the *range* of his territory, and the limitations on his *movements* within it'.

Children coming straight from home may be overwhelmed by the size of the building (Marshall 1988). Some children attend a nursery class in the same building as the school; others attend a nursery school or preschool close by or on the same site. Indeed, many children will have experienced a number of transitions prior to visiting school (DES 1990, para. 104). Some children 'may be attending a confusing multiplicity of forms of provision, in some cases concurrently, in others serially, as parents move area, jobs, or because each type of provision offers different facilities' (David 1990: 52).

Nevertheless, it should not be assumed that starting school is any easier for children who have experienced a number of settings than for those for whom this is their first transition (Dowling 1995).

Social discontinuities

Responding positively to the demands of the new environment and to different working practices depends to a large extent upon children's social and emotional well-being. The start of school involves children coping with a reorganisation of their identity and status from preschool child to school pupil. During this time they might find a social and cultural gap between preschool and school, there will be the challenge of becoming part of a new group, making new friends and, for some, the loss of friendships. Social interactions will be affected by:

- the physical layout of the classroom;
- having to relate to older pupils as well as children of a similar age;
- staffing ratios;
- the words and language of school that might be unfamiliar.

Philosophical discontinuities

Children bring their own experiences, skills, developmental differences, expectations and culture to school, therefore each transition is unique to the individual. For some children it may be the first time that they have been parted from the informal world of home, or had to leave their parents for any length of time to 'share' a strange adult with a number of other children. Others have experienced a range of different settings and encountered different people with different values in each. At school there may be:

- different approaches to teaching methods;
- a different balance of independent and group work;
- a different emphasis on work and play;
- more oral instruction;
- more emphasis on formal numeracy and literacy;
- restrictions on time;
- the need to use pencils and other small utensils, such as cutlery at lunchtime;
- a more structured timetable;
- more formal rules and classroom and institutional routines.

Not only do staff and children bring their own expectations to the induction, but there are also parental expectations of their children's learning and behaviour. This diversity of expectation may result in confusion for some children.

Acculturation

When children start school they are expected to modify their behaviour to fit the school culture. Some children find this difficult, others adjust quickly and others are passive recipients (Dowling 1995). Learning about learning at school, understanding the routines and language of school, and acquiring the culture take time. Helping children and their parents make sense of school and developing early home–school partnerships are seen as important factors in helping children to settle into school. Attitudes to learning are often dependent on children's social and emotional well-being. These two themes run throughout this book and are introduced briefly here.

Emotional well-being

Learning is dependent on the child's emotional state. 'Children need to feel secure and happy in order to deploy all their faculties fully to meet the challenges presented to them through the school curriculum' (Burrell and Bubb 2000). They also need to feel emotionally ready for school in order to meet new challenges with confidence (Goleman 1996). Self-esteem is a significant factor in being a successful learner and will affect the way in which children perceive their level of success (Ball 1994). If there is a lack of well-being, the child's development is likely to be threatened (Vandenbussche *et al.* 1994). Research has shown the correlation between high self-esteem and high academic achievement but even the most confident children can find the move to school intimidating, not feel in control and fear being wrong (Dowling 1995: 40). Some children are 'at risk' of not transferring well and develop problems caused by the stress of not settling in to school. If children cannot cope with the change of circumstances then they are unlikely to engage fully in the life of the class, may underperform academically and perhaps express frustration by demonstrating poor behaviour. Children need to be empowered at the start of their journey through school to overcome these anxieties and develop resilience which will give them a sense of mastery of their own lives.

Parents have a powerful effect on their child's sense of self-esteem, but when children start school it is the Reception class teacher who also influences that sense of identity. The first teacher has a role to play in developing children's self-esteem, with its resulting confidence, through giving them a feeling of belonging, self-worth and helping others accept them as competent and worthwhile. However, to attend to and value children fully puts a heavy responsibility on the Reception class teacher in a large class where there are few adults (Klein 1993).

Social well-being

Harmonious adaptation results from the child's ability to satisfy his or her own needs within the environment (Kienig 1997). One of these is the child's ability to establish social relations with other children and adults. However, differences in social skills may lead to differences in participation and opportunities to be actively involved. If children are socially skilled, they are more likely to have a succession of positive experiences with other children (Goleman 1996: 223) which, in turn, often brings a sense of well-being. Rutter (1997) suggests that it is the quality of the parents' relationship with each other that may influence the child's level of success in relationships with others.

There is a constantly shifting nature in children's relationships where opposing categories are common such as big and small, younger and older and where 'sometimes they are in a subordinate role, at other times they are superior or see themselves as equals' (Gura 1996: 36). Thus, children grow up and form their identities and define themselves in relation to the people with whom they are involved. Pollard states that their social development should, therefore, 'be seen as being symbiotic rather than just sequential, for each provides a vital element of the social context for the other' (Pollard 1996: 269).

A further aspect explored in this book is parents' involvement in their child's education to aid continuity. Nursery and Reception classes are well placed to encourage collaboration at the start of school which can continue throughout formal schooling. Having systems of induction for new children that aim to help them and their families become familiar with school, while helping teachers understand the children's background, is likely to motivate and encourage early learning and partnership. Important elements in establishing partnership are good communication skills and the frequency, amount, style and format of information given.

The start of school is only one transition that children make. Children experience a number of transitions during their school years, moving from one class to another, sometimes with different children, to a different teacher and to a different room. They also transfer between phases of education, for example from infants to juniors, and from primary to secondary. There are some who change schools with little notice and arrive mid-term. These transfers between schools are also looked at in this book. The negative effect of pupil mobility on confidence and learning highlights the need to help children develop skills of resilience to face uncertainty and reduce the impact of social and emotional turbulence.

The book concludes by looking at systems for monitoring and evaluating induction programmes. Evaluating the purposes, procedures and principles of induction helps to establish criteria for induction and systems for managing a programme of unhindered beginnings.

PART 1

Planning for the Start of School

CHAPTER 2

Admission

Key issues
- When do children start school?
- What are the implications for children born in the summer?
- What measures are being taken by authorities to ensure a seamless transition throughout childhood?

Children in the United Kingdom start their compulsory schooling earlier than their counterparts in the rest of Europe (Pugh 1996). The international norm is to start between the ages of five and seven, with the most common compulsory school starting age in Europe being six (European Commission 2000; Moss 2000). In England and Wales children are legally required to start school in the term following their fifth birthday, which is one of the lowest ages for school admission in Europe. In reality the actual school starting age is earlier still, with most children starting at four, because of the growing practice of admitting children to Reception class at the beginning of the year in which they become five (Sharp 1998). The only countries to start at a similar time are the Netherlands where most children enter school on a voluntary basis at four, and Luxembourg where attendance at nursery schooling is compulsory from four.

There is no clear educational or developmental rationale for children starting school in the term after their fifth birthday other than 'the accidental result of the exigencies of Parliamentary procedure and of general unconcern!' (Stretzer 1964 cited in Bennett and Kell 1989: 1). The age of five was first established as the school starting age in the 1870 Education Act, after some debate favouring six as the starting age. The main arguments put forward in favour of the earlier starting age emphasised the need to protect young children from exploitation and unhealthy conditions in the streets, while appeasing employers that an early start meant an earlier school leaving age, so children could enter the workforce at age 13 (Woodhead 1989). School, therefore, was seen as a way of serving adult needs rather than the needs of children.

But why continue to start school at this age? Certainly, there appears to be no compelling rationale for a statutory school age of five, or for the practice of admitting four-year-olds to school Reception classes (Sharp 1998). The government response to the Select Committee on Education and Employment (House of Commons 2001) agreed that the age of school entry was less important than the style of teaching employed when children enter school. The committee recommended that the compulsory school starting age should remain at the term after the child's fifth birthday with the Foundation Stage in England being fully implemented to ensure that children receive an informal style of education appropriate to their age. Children, therefore, will continue to be admitted to school early.

The fact that formal education begins at an increasingly younger age implies a sense of urgency, of hastening progress and of accelerating childhood (Nutbrown 1996). Nutbrown suggests that, rather than wanting the best for children, this acceleration to being grown up might be because childhood is less valued than adulthood. James and Prout (1997) follow a similar theme when they state that it is vital to focus on children not only as future-beings, but also as beings-in-the-present. Children are part of the socio-culture rather than in the process of becoming part of society, therefore teachers need to make the most of the moment and respect the pace of childhood.

> [F]or children it is *today* here, now, this minute that matters, but what we give them today must be made of the things *they need* today . . . There is a mischievous mistruth in the belief that doing certain things early helps children to get ready for the next stage. The best way to help a child to get ready to be five is to let her be three when she is three and let him be four when he is four . . . (Nutbrown 1996: 54)

Pascal (1990) and Williams (1998) state that starting school at four is potentially extremely stressful, particularly where school policy, provision and practice do not take into account developmental needs of young children.

> The child, the boy, the man, indeed, should know no other endeavour but to be at every stage of development wholly what this stage calls for. Then will each successive stage spring like a new shoot from a healthy bud; and, at each successive stage, he will with the same endeavour again accomplish the requirements of this stage: for only the adequate development of man at each preceding stage can effect and bring about adequate

✎ Activity 2.1

Look at your own setting and note some examples of hastening childhood. These might be social situations, the implementation of the curriculum or emotional expectations. How can developmental needs be met more fully?

development at each succeeding later stage. (Froebel 1887: 30, in Bruce *et al*. 1995: 16)

Across England and Wales there are a variety of entry policies including:

- annual intake usually in the September of the academic year in which the child's fifth birthday occurs;
- three intakes a year either in the term of their fifth birthday or the term following their fifth birthday;
- biannual intake usually in September and January in the half-year in which their fifth birthday occurs;
- daily on the child's fifth birthday.

In 1995, Sharp reported that the policies adopted for admitting children showed annual entry as the most common, followed by termly and biannual patterns. The former results in the youngest entrants starting school just after their fourth birthday. The Nursery Education Voucher Scheme exacerbated this in April 1997 as it had the effect of lowering the school starting age. Although it was withdrawn five months later on 31 August 1997, many local education authorities (LEAs) had by then extended the admission age downwards to accept children as soon as they reached the age of four, in order to get extra funding (Whitehead 1998). This increase of early entry to Reception classes was an unintentional result of the expansion of education for four-year-olds. More children, who, because of their age, are eligible for nursery education, are therefore now entering a system that was traditionally designed for children of five or above. Competition for pupils has also influenced this outcome. The combined effects of devolved funding, parental choice and the publication of league tables all conspire to make many schools want to attract new pupils as early as possible (Cleave and Brown 1993). Figures for the Annual School Census for January 1999 indicate that there are 56 per cent of four-year-olds in the Reception classes of maintained nursery classes and schools. There are now concerns that expansion plans mean that three-year-olds will be entering school. Wiltsher (2000) reported 1,146 three-year-olds in Reception classes in 1999. This is likely to be linked with the government aim to provide two-thirds of three-year-olds with a nursery place by 2002.

Annual admission is seen by many as being beneficial because it enables children to have three full years in infant school before assessment at seven (Cleave and Brown 1993). However, four-year-olds who attend school have significantly less experience of life than classmates of statutory school age and may therefore be at a disadvantage and are likely to lag behind their older peers for several years. The self-esteem of summer-born children could suffer because they are apparently less able than their classmates. There is no evidence to show that there is any educational or behavioural advantage linked to early school admission. Sharp (1998) concluded 'a later start appears not to be a disadvantage to children's progress'. Furthermore, she found that early entry to school for summer-born children did not result in higher achievement two or three years later (Sharp 1995). Indeed, Hughes *et al.* (1979) found that those children having difficulties on entry were still having problems four terms later. A gardening analogy identifies the irrationality of starting school without conditions being conducive to learning.

> **Gardeners** don't plant runner beans in January to get an earlier harvest **than their neighbours;** if they tried, they would probably get shrivelled **and stunted beans.** They fertilise the ground in the early months of the **year, so that when the beans are planted** – at the right time – they will flourish. (Oxfordshire County Council 1991 in Nutbrown 1996: 53)

Occasionally children may accelerate out of a stage in one particular aspect. Parents' right to defer entry has implications for later schooling as the child is placed with that age group throughout, even if they develop more rapidly later. However, flexibility in the school starting age, by delaying entry or admitting earlier, is likely to be beneficial. Prais (1997) raised the issue of a flexible school starting age when he found that primary classes in Switzerland contained over one in five children who were a year older than their chronological year group. This was largely the result of delayed entry, based on the recommendation of the kindergarten teachers (Sharp 1998). Crosser (1991) suggested that there are academic advantages to summer-born children from delayed entry, particularly in relation to boys' reading attainment. A study in the USA by Zill *et al.* (1997) showed that delayed entry was quite common, either because of teacher recommendation or because their parents believed that they were not ready for school. In general these were children who were younger in their age group and predominantly boys.

Since the introduction of the Foundation Stage in England, some authorities are trying to create a more cohesive and seamless system. The government has put a strong political emphasis on early years with the introduction of Early Years Development and Childcare Partnerships (EYDCP), the move to an integrated system of services and a National Childcare Strategy. This emphasises increased opportunities for all, eradication of child poverty and a commitment to improving children's educational achievement. In some cases authorities are reintroducing the start of formal full-time education at the beginning of the term after a child's fifth birthday. However, the compulsory start of school occurs part-way through the Foundation Stage. The National Curriculum is not compulsory until children begin Year 1 of Key Stage 1, when they are six. Moss (2001) advocates redefining the boundaries by moving the start of compulsory schooling to age six as it would contribute to viewing early childhood as a stage in its own right with its own identity.

CASE STUDY 2.1

The city of York is pioneering a new strategy to reverse the trend towards an earlier school starting age. They plan across departments integrating early education and childcare services to provide a unified service that has a holistic approach to young children and their families. The Early Years and Childcare Service, as a complete and discrete part of the authority structure, has overall responsibility for implementing the EYDCP Plan. The Partnership reviewed admissions policies to infant and primary schools and decided to adopt an option of children starting formal full-time education at the beginning of the term after their fifth birthday. This will be fully implemented by September 2003. (Osgood and Sharp 2000)

✎ **Activity 2.2**

Consider the admission policy in your authority. How does it fit with the structures set out in the EYDCP? The degree of integration of services, the frequency of admission and the starting point for summer-born children are points to get you started. Does an earlier start help children to learn more, sooner? Is there flexibility in the school starting age? Are there benefits for delayed entrants?

CHAPTER 3

Marketing the school

Key issues
- How do parents choose a school for their child?
- How can schools promote themselves?

Schools in England are set within a market system of parental choice, open enrolment, devolved budgets and formula funding where parents have rights to choose a school for their child to attend. The idea of an education market was established by the provisions of the Education Reform Act 1988 and given reinforcement by the 1993 Act (Gewirtz *et al.* 1995). The implication is that parents should be consumers as well as partners who will make considered choices between schools on the basis of a careful and well-informed comparison of each school's educational philosophy, policies and performance. However, this market place culture may cause confusion when parents consider which school they want their child to attend, as the following case study reveals.

CASE STUDY 3.1

This correspondence between Lorraine and her mum takes place when Lorraine starts looking for a school for her daughter.

Dear 'Granny',
   I'm in the most frightful dilemma! We've just had a letter from the school near the library telling us that Stacey is starting school there after Easter. Her friend Samantha is going to the other school and we'd thought she'd be going there with her. Now we don't know what to do. My understanding was that it's the school for this area. It has a good name – we even moved here because it has such a good reputation! I can remember the estate agent telling us that several people had moved here because of the school.

Stacey's white rabbit . . .
Lorraine

Dear Lorraine,

You're not to worry so much, but you must get the right school because getting a good start is so important, isn't it? I had a leaflet through the door the other day that said, 'you can say which school you would prefer your child to go to'. [DFE 1994: 9]. I don't think your dad and I could do that for you when you started. You'll need to go and look at both schools and make up your own mind which one is right for you and Stacey. Pick the school with care and match Stacey to the school, rather than match the school that you want, to her.

Your dad said . . .
Mum

Dear 'Granny',

You were absolutely right about going to look. The only problem was that we didn't really know what to look for or what to ask! We looked at both schools and spent an hour in each. We went to the school by the library first of all but I don't think she could cope with the headmaster; he would put her off for life! She's got to like him. Anyway, the headmaster at the other school was ever so nice. He gave us a pamphlet about the school and showed us round and the teacher of the little ones was lovely. We liked the feel of the place and all the children seemed happy. Anyway, it's slightly nearer than the other one and we've heard lots of good things about it.

Stacey's getting very excited about going . . .
Lorraine

(Adapted from Fabian 1998)

A code of practice applying to school admissions came into force in September 2000 which requires LEAs to make arrangements to enable parents of children in their area to express a preference as to their choice of school (Ofsted 1999a). However, the above case study raises a number of issues that need consideration:

- parents knowing they have a choice;
- availability of places;
- children being separated from friends due to parental choice;
- parents knowing what to ask and what to look for in their choice;
- parents judging a school on reputation, staff personalities or feel.

Choosing a school

Education markets are localised and need to be viewed in context. For example, there may be competition from other schools with purpose-built nursery facilities. Since the 1980 Education Act all schools have been required to provide information for parents and publish a prospectus or brochure 'which describes its achievements and what it has to offer' (DFE 1994: 7). The school prospectus is a key document in informing parents about the school but, in addition, the quality of work and achievements can be demonstrated through:

- press releases;
- children's work on display locally, e.g. in the library or shopping centre;
- curriculum evenings for prospective parents;
- invitations to school assemblies, open evenings or concerts;
- information sent to prospective parents;
- the behaviour of the pupils who represent the school in the community every day.

Lack of knowledge about what it is that they need to know in order to evaluate schools may make it difficult for parents to choose a school for their child. Parents' first impressions are likely to be based on the physical environment and the work and notices on display which set the general tone. If parents are to make an informed decision about choosing a school, increasingly head teachers are expected to explain the systems and show them the school during any pre-registration visits in order for them to:

- see the way that learning takes place;
- understand the way discipline is handled;
- gain a sense of the school's ethos;
- see the state of the building and level of resources;
- be satisfied with the security arrangements.

Hubberstey (1994) suggests that parents conduct some research about possible schools for their child and visit a number of schools to ask the head teacher questions. However, some aspects of a school can elude all but the most searching enquiry and the answers may hold little meaning for those who are unsure about what it is they are looking for in a school. Dowling (1995: 15) points out 'in some areas parents have little awareness of their opportunity for choice and, even if they do, they lack the time, energy or finance for transport to exercise it'.

Parents choose a school for their child for more than one reason, although most parents choose a particular school because of the geographical location (Hughes *et al.* 1994). This suggests that many parents make a choice of convenience as it is the nearest school or because the school is part of the local community. For some parents the choice of school is not an issue, simply because they have chosen it for their firstborn and their subsequent children then attend the same school. Some parents have much older children who attended a school, or attended it themselves, and still choose the school for their younger children (Hughes *et al.* 1994). For others it is important that their children are with their friends and they choose a school for this reason.

Often parents choose a school because of its 'good reputation' but they are not always clear about what this means except they want to send their children there, and have done so for a number of years. Some information about the school is gained by word of mouth. However, one enthusiastic or disillusioned parent can distort a school's reputation, as the information may be undeserved or out of date and not necessarily bear any reference to recent experience.

Increasingly, parents are turning to the Office for Standards in Education (Ofsted) inspection evidence for additional information about the school. League tables of Standard Assessment Tests (SATs) results help parents make direct comparisons between schools in their area, although these often require considerable interpretation.

Some parents stand outside the school and watch how it operates at the beginning and end of the day and at break times. For those who look around the school before deciding, they also make their choice on the ethos of the school. Hay (1997: 120) suggests that parents will want:

- to feel a welcoming atmosphere;
- to see children taking a positive pride in their work and play;
- to see positive relationships between staff/children, children/children and staff/staff.

Quality is perceived as levels of head teacher and staff involvement, the approachability of the Reception class teacher(s) and the apparent genuineness of staff in caring for children. Choosing a school therefore might be to do with the nature of the people whom parents come into contact with at the school rather than its academic results.

Schools may need to emphasise their appreciation of children's individuality rather than the school's performance. Other criteria might be to do with values:

> representation in terms of race, ethnicity, gender and disability can provide important indicators for parents concerned both about the value which a childcare setting places on diversity, and for the development of self-esteem and self-perceptions of those children who might attend (Brophy and Statham 1994: 69)

Each factor is not necessarily interlinked, nor do parents necessarily make choices in a logical way, listing criteria in a hierarchical fashion. Choice clearly has 'messy, multidimensional, intuitive and seemingly irrational or non-rational elements' (Gewirtz *et al.* 1995: 6). It is made within a social context and is influenced by a family's cultural and ethnic values.

Not all parents are looking for the same thing and their choice is often based on instinct rather than logic. In reality, therefore, parents may choose to send their child to a school, not for its academic record but for other criteria such as the school's ability to allow each child his or her uniqueness, their child's happiness, because of established friendships, because there is no choice geographically, because it is their nearest or because of the school's perceived reputation.

✎ Activity 3.1

Schools may need to treat potential parents as partners even before their children begin school and educate parents about their school before they begin to contemplate schools for their children.

- How might the reputation of a school be disseminated?
- What takes place at pre-registration? For example, an individual tour of the school, time for questions, written information in the form of the school prospectus.
- Many parents are not sure what to look for or what to ask when viewing a school. What information are parents likely to want to know about your school? What sort of things are particular to your school which will help to convince parents of its worth?

CHAPTER 4

Expectations and preparations

Key issues
- How do children view school?
- How do parents approach the start of school?

Before children enter school there are uncertainties and expectations about the future. The experience of going to school can also be a significant event for parents. They have a complexity of emotions which range from positive feelings of anticipation of developmental benefits for their child, to feelings of apprehension and worry about this unknown experience. For some parents it may be the first time that they have placed the care of their child in the hands of another adult. This can lead to vulnerabilities about needing to trust their child in someone else's care as well as trusting another adult with their child. For others the start of school might be seen as a significant life-change not only in their child's life but in theirs, too. The introduction of a significant adult in the form of a teacher into their lives marks a turning point in the relationship between parent(s) and child (Burtscher 1997). Therefore the start of school is a time of psychological and social change not only for the child, but also for each family member. The subsequent network of friends and the quality of family relationships may, as a result, change both for children and adults.

Children's perspective

Children have different approaches to school. For some, school is an unknown adventure to look forward to with excitement. For others, it can be a potentially frightening place, whether or not they have had preschool experience. However, before starting school most children are looking forward to going even though they are unclear about its physical aspects, what it entails or the role of the teacher. Griebel and Niesel (2000) found that children only had a vague idea about what to expect, were nervous and insecure but were also convinced that they were going to do well. Those things that children look forward to include: 'being big'; having an approachable teacher; choosing from a wider variety of resources than at preschool; the novelty of new activities; making new friends, although some children worry that they might not know anyone at first (Adapted from Fabian 1998).

CASE STUDY 4.1

The following conversation between a father and his two children indicates some of the things that children look forward to, as well as some misconceptions about school.

Dad: Are you looking forward to going to school, Hayley?

Hayley: Ooh! Yes!

Dad: Do you know what happens there?

Hayley: I don't know. Mm, it's like preschool.

James: No, it's not, you only play at preschool and you don't do any work. We get loads of work to do at school. We go all day. Preschool is for little children. School's bigger and there's more things to play with. School's got drawers and water and preschool hasn't. And it's the same 'cos we've got a home corner and they've got a home corner. You'll learn about reading and writing and PE and . . .

Hayley: What's PE?

James: It's when you take your clothes off and climb ladders and things.

Hayley: Is that what the ladders are for? I thought they were for the builders when the school's old – to mend it.

Dad: What do you think a teacher does, Hayley?

Hayley: She tells you what to do and learns you stuff. She'll learn me how to write and how to read. You've got to do your homework every day. There'll be pencils and paper and she'll talk about the letters on the wall. Will there be books there?

Dad: Yes, lots of books, like the ones that James brings home.

James: My first reading book didn't have any words in it! My first work was a little bit of writing but I couldn't write much letters down. I thought I'd just be playing with things when I first went. I was really happy that I was in school. When we started with the computer I thought I had to put it on and it would do it by itself, but it didn't! But the big ones told me. Now I'm six I know how to do things. It was fun.

It's still fun! In Reception we did painting and drawing and sand. I really wanted to find sand there. You go to learn things. You've got to learn, haven't you?

Look! I've finished my picture. I was little then, now I'm taller. I'm much happier now. When I first went I was terrified of not having any friends, now I'm not because I've got new friends, I know everyone now. When I started I was quiet but now I like to talk a lot. I can ride without stabilisers now. I'm big now.

Hayley: I'll be big when I go to big school.

James: No, you won't: you'll be one of the little ones!

(Adapted from Fabian 1998)

✎ Activity 4.1

Ask the children in your care about their views of school before they started. It is sometimes useful for them to draw a picture of how they felt before they came to school. What was their understanding of school? What were they looking forward to and what were their concerns?

As the start of school approaches, children sometimes see school in terms of their lunch box, uniform and PE kit rather than learning. A survey of children starting school by Barrett (1986) tells of ways that parents tried to prepare their children for the approach of school by talking about it and shopping for new 'shoes, bags or other clothing especially bought, made and labelled for school' (Barrett 1986: 28). Many children rehearse trying on their uniform, doing up buttons, buckling shoes and playing with their new bag. Brown and Cleave (1994: 3), however, point out that starting school 'is not just about having a new school bag and arriving at the beginning of the new term'. These are only the outward physical preparations. If children have pre-entry visits, this gives them some insight, although many children view the start of school as the time when these visits begin, rather than from the time they are registered full-time, particularly if they have had several visits before starting.

Those with older brothers and sisters already at school sometimes play at 'schools'. They gain an understanding of the nature of school through listening to their older siblings, accompanying them to school each day or seeing school items, such as books that are brought home. Children are also influenced by adult messages but sometimes the teacher is used as a threat as well as a support. For example, children are told 'what will the teacher think if you behave like this?' (Griebel and Niesel 1999).

CASE STUDY 4.2

The following illustrates some of the preparations that two parents made as their children approached the start of school. We can see that they are looking for ways of helping their children to learn and to help them gain knowledge that will be valuable. There is a need for guidance, because even in schools with informative induction procedures, parents are still unsure what is educative (Fabian 1996).

Alison: We've talked a lot about it as a family and been on a special shopping trip to buy the uniform. I put his nametags in and he's practised trying it on and we've videoed him. He wanted an alarm clock so we bought him one and he practised getting up early.

Graham: We've read books about school to Sophie and talked to her about what it will be like. We've read some books for us too, which gave suggestions for things we could do at home. We've walked past school and learnt the route. We've taken any opportunities to go and see it, for example there was a fête we went to. We had her friends round who are starting with her, and worked our way through the exercises in some educational books we bought. But it would be nice to talk to parents who went up last year who could tell us what to do and expect. Those with older brothers and sisters have an advantage – I don't see any problems with our younger one starting.

Alison: Yes, I agree. But I also feel I need help in helping him with things like writing and learning the alphabet. I think we've done it all wrong and I won't know until he starts school.

Graham: Yes, in some respects it would be helpful to have information before she starts. We need to know at an early stage the basic information on what the school wants us to do, things like the way they do the alphabet, advice on the style of writing and so on. What books they recommend. There are so many on the market, there's too much choice. Children want to learn at a much earlier stage and we're not sure what's best. In the library, we're not sure which books to work from. It would've been helpful if we'd had a list of books, which would tie in with the first books at school. Like Alison said, you don't want them to start and then be told 'you should have done these things 12 months ago'.

(Adapted from Fabian 1998)

Parents' perspective

The beginning of school is seen as important for the child's whole school career. The 'seriousity' of life starts with school, and consequently the family atmosphere is likely to get stricter as school approaches (Griebel and Niesel 1999). Items of news about school reported in the media alert parents to wider aspects of education that they might not have considered previously, for example, school organisation and teachers' pay and conditions. Issues are sometimes reported that might give cause for concern such as pupils' behaviour, aspects of the curriculum and school closures. This, along with recollections from their own school days, often forms parents' perceptions of school for their first child.

Most parents are concerned about their child's well-being at the start of school and are sometimes anxious about what change might bring. The issues that most concern parents are that their children should acquire skills, knowledge and values that they believe to be important (Tizard and Hughes 1984), the ratio of adults to children, and playtime and lunch-time (Dowling 1988; Cleave and Brown 1991). Other concerns include:

- the challenge of older children;
- larger numbers of children to relate to;
- loss of their child's individuality and uniqueness;
- their child's ability to cope;
- pressure of the literacy and numeracy hours;
- baseline assessment;
- how to prepare their child for school;
- their child's friendships;
- bullying;
- school security.

Parents want their child to be confident (Dowling 2000: 1). They want their child to be 'normal' and know what to do, and are sometimes surprised at how well their children cope. They have expectations that the teacher will care for their child, give them support and ensure they succeed. Dalli (1999) explores some issues surrounding parents' expectations with regard to developmental benefits of childcare. In her stories of mothers of children starting childcare, she found there was an expectation that starting would enable children to interact with more people and gain from the social stimulation of a group, meet their child's need to be stimulated cognitively and encourage their child to rely on more than one person.

Parents have an influence on their child's levels of confidence during the transition. Indeed, parental confidence is the key to much of their child's success (Pugh *et al.* 1994). Parents are more likely to feel confident if they know the systems in school, have an understanding of the 'language', are aware of the curriculum areas and can recognise key staff. They want 'to do it right' and help their child through the unexpected such as having a supply teacher for the day. However, there is a danger that the picture that parents give their children of school does not live up to expectations, and children are left to handle the difference between the rhetoric and the reality (Dunlop 2001).

Many parents expect the first day to go well but are anxious beforehand that all should continue to go well as the days and weeks pass. An aspect that they think might hasten the expectation that it will 'all end in tears' is their child's realisation that school is all day, every day and 'forever'. Indeed, the build-up to school can be so intense in some families that children might not realise that there will still be a life outside school for family events like swimming or holidays.

There are several demands on parents when their child first begins school, not least because of the changes to the balance of family life. Some no longer feel in control of their child's development, their own cultural influence and their level of involvement with their child. Some feel jealous that the teacher comes to know their child better than they do. Much of the worry stems from the fact that parents feel they have to put their trust in others (Fabian 1996).

✎ **Activity 4.2**

Parents often help their child to prepare for school by looking at children's storybooks about starting school. Some books present pictures about activities at school and the teacher's role; some demonstrate the way children might feel about starting school; others depict a 'typical' school day. Look at some children's books about starting school and evaluate the messages that they are giving to parents and their children about school.

PART 2
Preparing Schools for Children

CHAPTER 5

The role of the induction coordinator

Key issues
- Who manages the induction programme?
- What skills and qualities are needed to be an effective induction coordinator?
- How is the induction programme managed?

Schools need to consider who will use any information about starting school that is given, as it is not only the children who need a good start to school but their parents, too. A fundamental question is whether children should be prepared for, and adapted to, school or the school for the children. A school that is prepared for receiving children is a school that is able to see the child's perspective, understand the child's needs and create an appropriate learning environment, while recognising the importance of developing and maintaining a partnership with parents. 'Child-ready' schools receive children knowing about individuals and having given children and their parents an understanding of the school (Brostrom 2000). This comes about through a well-planned induction programme and clear communication. Even in the smallest school a team leader is needed to manage the programme and ensure that the various experiences of home, preschool and school are connected into a cohesive whole for each child.

Who is the coordinator?

The role of the induction coordinator is not always seen as a separate one and is often subsumed within other duties. It can be a joint responsibility or carried out by one person, perhaps the head teacher, Reception class teacher, early years coordinator or deputy head teacher. The following case study outlines two examples.

CASE STUDY 5.1

At one infant school, the head teacher managed the induction. She found that she was able to get to know the families and avert any problems before they occurred. She saw the induction as 'beginning the partnership before they come through the door. I can begin to establish a purposeful relationship and they see where I'm coming from. It's taken the sting out of some situations.' She saw the visits to school as helping children and parents to feel welcome and for them to begin to understand 'what school is about these days, to get a feeling of the regime and the opportunities that children bring with them'. Children and parents did not meet any of the four Reception class teachers until the last in a series of six visits.

At a primary school, the head teacher considered that induction was better handled by one of the Reception class teachers, and had appointed her as the induction coordinator. Although she was responsible for the induction programme, the head teacher was involved with talking to parents on the initial visit that they made to school. The coordinator saw induction as establishing a home–school link where parents can 'see a warm, friendly environment and that we, as teachers, are approachable and human'. She and the other Reception class teacher felt that a good induction is crucial for children to gain an insight into the social aspects of school, meet other children and their teacher, dispel any fears and feel confident to leave their parents.

(Adapted from Fabian 1998)

Key personal skills

There is general agreement (Everard and Morris 1996; Goleman 1998; Bell and Ritchie 1999) about the personality characteristics and social skills needed for such a management role. The following key interpersonal skills embrace important qualities of attitude and commitment needed to fulfil the role successfully:

- to empathise with others, show concern and be sensitive to their emotional state;
- to act consistently;
- to maintain hope, belief and optimism;
- to want success for the programme and children's start to school;
- to be willing to question practice and take risks;
- to anticipate, and accept, possible consequences of actions;
- to develop the capacity to accept, deal with and use conflict constructively;

- to develop self-awareness, identify and state one's own feelings, have a good self-image and be resilient;
- to cultivate a tolerance for ambiguity and complexity and avoid viewing issues in black and white;
- to be an active listener, who is perceptive and can interpret meanings;
- to communicate clearly, talk in positive, supportive terms and summarise concisely;
- to understand how learning about a new situation takes place;
- to accept others in a non-judgemental way.

Aspects of the coordinator's role

Managing the induction of the new intake effectively involves:

- monitoring and evaluating the policy and programme;
- improving the induction policy and programme;
- managing the resources of time, staff and budget;
- leading the Reception class team on induction issues;
- developing and reviewing a school view of the nature of induction, including relevant professional development and induction for pupils with special educational needs;
- facilitating and monitoring the children's introduction to the classroom;
- inter-settings liaison and links with other agencies, parents and the community;
- awareness of wider issues to do with induction such as parents' concerns about security, bullying and substance abuse;
- monitoring children's settling-in progress;
- promoting the school's interests;
- managing the procedure for admitting children;
- keeping up to date with current developments and issues about transitions.

The role of the coordinator comprises managing before, during and after new children start school.

✎ **Activity 5.1**

Try and write a job description for the induction coordinator. It might be that the role is subsumed within the role of the Foundation Stage/Key Stage 1 coordinator. The following might help to get you started.

Role	Task
Evaluator	• Assess attainment on entry • Identify strengths and areas for development

Strategic development	• Advise about targets for improvement • Update and implement the induction policy • Update early years curriculum guidelines • Facilitate parental involvement
Resource management	• Organise purchasing of resources, e.g. starting school video
Staff development	• Hold staff development meetings to assist colleagues' understanding of induction
Monitor	• Monitor children's introduction and settling in to school • Monitor pupils' learning • Monitor practitioners' planning • Visit classrooms to evaluate the quality of learning
Develop personal in-service training (INSET) needs	• Keep up to date with local and national developments about admission and induction • Attend early years courses and conferences • Liaise with other schools • Attend cluster working groups

Purpose of induction

What is important at the start of school? It is useful to explore this from the perspective of the school, the parents and the children. Figure 5.1 outlines the needs of the main stakeholders.

Dowling has identified the important features of successful induction:

- for all parents to become aware of the educational value of life in the home;
- to understand the significance of the playgroup, nursery and Reception curriculums and how each contributes to their child's subsequent well-being and achievement;
- for preschool staffs to become familiar with the curriculum and organisation offered and the expectations of children in Reception classes;
- to identify sources of match and mismatch with their own provisions;
- for teachers to gain as full a picture as possible of each child's past experiences, interests and achievements prior to starting school;
- to recognise, respect and support the vital role that parents and carers play in their child's progress and development; and

- for all parties to recognise the value of working in harmony to support the child.

(Dowling 1995: 19–20)

Children	Parents	School
• To become familiar with the physical layout of school • To gain an understanding of the nature of learning in school by participating in activities • To get to know the teacher and his or her expectations • To begin to feel at home • To experience significant events of the day such as assembly, lunch-time and playtime • To know that his or her behaviour is understood • To know that he or she is known	• To become familiar with the physical layout of school • To get to know the teacher and his or her expectations • To receive verbal and written information about the school, the curriculum, their responsibilities, health and safety issues • To meet staff • To meet other parents and develop support systems • To gain an understanding of school by comparing with preschool • To know how to become involved with school (social events, supporting learning) • To know how feedback will be gained	• To gain information about individual children and their families • To give information • To ensure that children have a pleasant experience of school • To make links with preschool • To begin to develop a partnership with parents

Figure 5.1 What the main stakeholders need during induction

Planning the programme

If the purposes of an induction programme are orientation, information sharing, meeting others and gaining an understanding of the school, then there is a need to understand the implications for practice. For example:

- If children and parents are going to have a taste of school, what experiences will give them an indication of the nature of learning?
- If visits are to help children form the beginning of friendships, then what activities are likely to encourage this?
- If children are to experience social events that are new to them such as lunch-time, playtime and assembly, how can this be introduced best?

In a study carried out for The Ministry of Education in Denmark, Brostrom (2000) identified 32 transition activities that 249 preschool and school staff were using, as outlined in Figure 5.2.

Transition activity	Percentage of schools doing these
1. The school invites the child to visit the class before school starts	95.9
2. The preschool teachers and children visit the class before school starts	93.4
3. The preschool teachers and children visit leisure time centre	93.1
4. The next year teacher spends time in the kindergarten class	92.3
5. Talk with parents after school starts	90.0
6. Preschool teachers and kindergarten teachers have conferences before school starts about children's lives and development	89.9
7. Letters to parents before school starts	89.3
8. Flyers to parents before school starts	87.6
9. The teaching team in kindergarten is made up of pedagogues and teachers	86.5
10. Letters to children before school starts	85.2
11. Open house in kindergarten class before school starts	84.9
12. Some teaching periods are coordinated between kindergarten class, Grades 1–2 and leisure time centre	83.9
13. Meetings with children and parents before school starts	83.0
14. Talks with parents before school starts	82.0
15. Cooperation with parents is coordinated between school and leisure time centre	81.9
16. Kindergarten, school and leisure time centre read each others' curriculum, activity plans and other written documents	80.1
17. Kindergarten teachers visit their forthcoming pupils in their preschools	79.8
18. Leisure time teachers are a part of the teacher team in school	79.2
19. Kindergarten teachers follow the children to Grade 1	78.3
20. The school invites the eldest children in preschools to participate in cultural events at school	77.6
21. At school enrolment children and parents meet the kindergarten teacher	77.6
22. Teachers and pedagogues visit each other and observe the educational practice	77.2
23. Teachers and pedagogues have shared meetings to discuss education	76.0
24. Letters to parents after school starts	71.1
25. Before school starts preschool and kindergarten classes have a shared meeting with parents	65.7
26. Coordinated curriculum between preschool, kindergarten class and leisure time centre	60.3
27. Coordinated teaching between preschool, kindergarten class and leisure time centre	59.4
28. Open house in kindergarten class after the school starts	52.8
29. Flyer to parents after school starts	41.1
30. Home visits after school starts	40.0
31. Letters to children after school starts	39.6
32. Home visit before school starts	27.5

Figure 5.2   Percentage of schools doing transition activities

The activities in Figure 5.2 can be grouped into five categories:

- liaison between adults in settings;
- information sharing between staff, and between staff and parents;
- information giving;
- experience of settings and people;
- development of structures where teaching groups work together.

Where does the coordinator begin? The above list raises issues about the appropriateness of transitional activities. What is needed in one situation may not work in another. Each programme needs to be right for the local circumstances and flexible enough to meet different needs. Apart from the range of transition activities, there are a number of people to consider when planning a programme:

- parents – both new and those with children already at the school;
- children – both new and those already in the class;
- preschool children and staff;
- children with special educational needs;
- children with English as an additional language;
- staff at the school.

Some of the activities such as preschool liaison will be continuous, whereas others such as inviting a speaker to talk to parents are individual activities. Effective transition programmes prepare preschoolers for the challenges and demands of school. They usually:

- occur prior to and during the transition period;
- are systematic and clearly planned, while allowing for flexibility;
- are collaborative, involving adults from preschool, school and home;
- are individualised.

The design is most likely to be successful if it takes into account:

- the amount of time and finance allocated;
- timing;
- the number of transitional experiences to be included;
- the way in which information is shared.

Figure 5.3 outlines the stages in managing the programme.

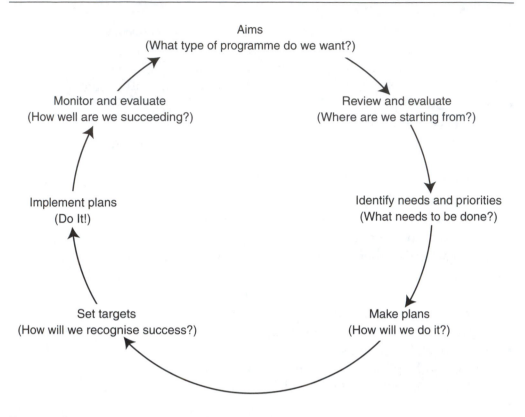

Figure 5.3 A planning cycle for an induction programme

✎ Activity 5.2

Put together the first part of your induction programme using the framework in Figure 5.3 of aims, review, priorities, plans and targets. Consider what you want from the programme, what happens already, and how you will meet the needs of children and parents. Consider when your induction procedure starts. Is it:

- the year before entry?
- the term before entry?
- a few weeks before entry?

Why is this the best time?

Barriers to effective programmes

A well thought-out transition programme indicates a school's commitment to the success of its pupils. However, a structured programme in itself is insufficient. By developing a culture and ethos that lends itself to a framework of support, children will be encouraged to think, develop and continue learning. Some of the perceived barriers to implementing transition programmes, identified by Brostrom (2000), included the following:

- lack of time/resources;
- too many preschools with which to liaise;
- difference in educational cultures;
- professional or union boundaries;
- mutual lack of interest, reluctance or aversion;
- time taken from the children;
- too many children involved;
- too much pressure on parents, parents not interested;
- class lists established too late.

Brostrom (2000) outlines how a similar survey involving 3,595 American kindergarten teachers (Pianta *et al.* 1999) found the following results:

- class lists established too late 55 per cent
- lack of time 37 per cent
- lack of resources 36 per cent
- too much pressure on parents or parents not interested 31 per cent
- mutual lack of interest, reluctance and aversion 9 per cent

Communication skills

Adopting the appropriate level of discussion is vital in giving parents and children confidence. The main ways of communicating with parents are through speaking and written documentation. Each of the following elements has a value in transmitting a message:

- words 7 per cent
- tone 35 per cent
- non-verbal or body language 58 per cent

(Hay 1997: 72)

Effective listening is part of successful communication. It entails hearing the words, thinking about their meaning and planning the response quickly (Bleach 1999). Another important aspect of successful communication is the flow, amount, style and format of any information given. Information and school values can be made accessible through stories, videos, photographs, slides, and parent and pupil presentations. The point at which information is given and the amount are critical to harmony.

✎ **Activity 5.3**

Consider how to:

- give parents and staff information about the induction process;
- give parents details of how to help their children through the induction;
- give information in an accessible way;
- help parents to ask questions;
- help parents to inform the school about their child in a way that is easy for them.

Parents want sufficient information and opportunities to understand the school environment, its curriculum and systems. Most share this with their child and develop their understanding together. However, when information is substantial or given very rapidly, or the terminology used is unfamiliar, then it is confusing, causes anxiety and hinders the induction process. Information given during induction visits that is accessible both in quality and quantity helps parents in their understanding, gives them confidence and reduces stress. Where insufficient information is given, it leads to parental anxiety and, in turn, affects their child's ability to 'settle'. Misunderstanding can also cause anxiety. The induction to school is likely to be improved, therefore, by the appropriate quantity and content of information passed to parents. Well-informed parents are less likely to be stressed about their child's transition to school and more able to assist their child in overcoming any confusion and frustration and in adapting to the new environment (Bredekamp 1987).

✎ **Activity 5.4**

It is important to get the flow and amount of information at a level that is easily digestible. Consider the following case study of visits to two different schools, and decide which parent found information more easily accessible on their first visit. How would you conduct the first meeting of new parents and children?

CASE STUDY 5.2

Lorraine and Debbie visit schools.

Lorraine: Hi Debbie, it's Lorraine. I thought I'd just phone and tell you about Stacey's visit to school and see how Hayley got on.

Debbie: Oh, the children don't go the first time. All the parents went into the hall at two o'clock and that lovely secretary gave us a big envelope that had loads of forms to fill in. There was tea and biscuits and, oh yes, the sweatshirts were all laid out for us to buy.

Lorraine: Ours was very different. I feel Stacey's going to be in good hands. I took her with me and it was lovely walking in 'cos the head teacher and the teacher were there to meet us in the hall. The teacher seemed to know all the children and it made you feel confident. There were only a few of us and we sat down and then the children went with the teacher to the classroom. The head talked to us about PE kit, school uniform and lunch-time. He wants us to come and help in the classroom if we want to.

Debbie: Yes, we had some of that about wanting us to help in school. First she told us about all these forms. The white card was for the school card index, the white forms for when Hayley goes on visits, the blue form was something to do with the government. Then there was the school prospectus . . .

Lorraine: Yes, we had one of those

Debbie: . . . and the preschool booklet, and she said that the preschool profile was to come, and another booklet on the last visit.

Lorraine: Wow, what a lot of forms and things. With ours, the teacher came back and talked to us about what they wanted the children to be able to do. About writing their name and saying the letters, and they gave us a sheet with letters and pictures on. She told us about a book that we could write in that's kept with their reading book and said it was so they could write messages to us, too. She told us about the reading scheme and showed us some books.

Debbie: We're not going to get that until the last afternoon. That's when Hayley meets her teacher. The headmistress said she'd show us a video and tell us about how we can help with reading. This time she talked about us being partners and about the things in the prospectus. She talked very fast so I can't remember all of it now, but there was something about catching children doing well and she talked about all the subjects and fitting them together as themes and if something didn't fit, doing it separately, like maths.

Lorraine: Yes, we had something on maths; she showed us something she called 'multi-link' and how they use things like that instead of copying out of books. Then somebody asked a question about medicines.

Debbie: Oh, we had something about health and safety and about school meals and Friends of the School and how they've got a couple of parent reps for each class. I knew about that because Sheila did that when James first started. Then one of the governors talked to us and someone from the school health service.

Lorraine: Oh! Really? We were shown round the school to see what they do. It gave me a feel for the place. If you don't know anything about a school, you go in like a piece of blotting paper. We went to the classroom to collect the children and they were having a story.

Debbie: We haven't seen the classroom yet but we'll go to school every other Monday for the rest of this term and go into a room with some of the other children who are starting in the summer. It's not her proper classroom; we'll see that later. Look, I must dash now, see you next week.

(Adapted from Fabian 2000)

Developing written materials

Written communication should be clear, readable, relevant and informative (Hay 1997: 75). It also needs to be sensitive to, and address, changing needs, interests and concerns. All schools have a school prospectus and many have a separate brochure for parents of children who are just starting school. If schools have a programme of pre-entry visits then parents will have received some of the information orally, but it is always useful to have this in written format, both for those who are unable to attend the meetings and for referring to at a later date.

Many schools have discovered the marketing value of an attractive and informative booklet but the tone they set is as important as the information, so parents do not feel patronised, overwhelmed or demoralised. Clear, succinct and comprehensive documentation is important if parents are going to be able to access it without difficulty. In the desire to include everything, there is danger of information overload. However, in striving to inform parents, uniformity might be denying differences. If parents think that they or their children do not match the norm, they might think that they will be seen as problematic. Educational inclusion is as much about perceptions as it is about access. The expectations of children and parents are different in different cultures so written material needs to take into account the differences and be made accessible to all parents by writing it in appropriate languages and with the appropriate emphasis.

Many schools are now putting information about the induction to school on their web sites or communicating it by email. However, email has a number of inherent difficulties:

* perceived impersonality and a sense of anonymity;
* the context and climate are lacking, therefore the writer is working in a void;

- lack of immediate feedback through body language;
- misunderstandings, as individual words may contain greater significance than intended or be interpreted in different ways.

The advantages are:

- greater accessibility for working parents;
- it is perceived as up to date;
- the immediacy of updating information on the web site.

✎ **Activity 5.5**

Many schools involve pupils in developing booklets and web sites that inform parents and new children about the start of school. Look at your starting-school booklet and information on your school web site about starting school.

- What does it include?
- Why is each aspect included?
- Is the format accessible? Is it easy to navigate?
- What involvement do the current pupils have in producing the information?
- How might it be viewed from the point of view of a minority group parent (for example, a single parent, a disabled child's parent, a parent whose child speaks English as an additional language)?

CHAPTER 6

Transition activities

Key issues
- How do schools ensure that children and their parents gain an understanding of school?
- How do schools learn about individual children?

Schools vary in the amount and content of transitional activities that they provide, with many schools having a combination of activities to ensure a good transfer to school for pupils and their parents. This might involve single visits; a series of half-day visits; talks to parents during an afternoon or evening; parents staying with their child; parents leaving their child with the teacher; and experience of lunch-time and the playground. This chapter takes some of the transitional activities outlined in Chapter 5 and looks at them in more depth. Mutual visits between school and preschool groups usually form part of the induction programme and these are explored further in Chapter 8. Home visiting is a feature of some schools' induction programmes and can help teachers gain an insight into children's levels of attainment. This is looked at in Chapter 9.

Visits to school

Meetings and visits prior to starting school can help to dispel some of the anxiety that children and their families may feel (Dowling 1995). To develop a sense of security, children and their parents need time and opportunities to become acquainted with the school accommodation, the people and routines. Visits are also an opportunity for staff to observe and build up a picture of each child.

Schools might want to question the purpose of any preliminary visits that they offer and look at them from the parents' and children's perspectives. What message about the school is received? The way that visits are conducted is critical if the child's emotional well-being is to be supported. Some systems might be unintentionally misguiding or unhelpful. Visits can sometimes disrupt established classes, so the size and timing of the visiting group needs careful consideration.

Schools may also want to question the format that the visits take and whether the induction itself inhibits the transition. Is the expectation and excitement of starting school removed in the frustration of short visits and 'dabbling toes' rather than jumping straight in? Are elaborate induction procedures necessary? What helps in the long term? It is the quality of preliminary visits rather than the quantity that is important. High-quality experiences in a calm atmosphere with opportunities to see what school is about, are more likely to be successful than overcrowded visits where the teacher feels flustered.

Familiarisation with the physical surroundings

One of the most important influences on learning is the context. If the setting is familiar, children are likely to feel comfortable and can use their skills, knowledge and past experiences more easily to make sense of new activities. Cleave and Brown (1991) suggest that the previous experiences that children bring with them need to be taken into account on any pre-entry visits and that for some children, school seems an 'alien place'. Some children will have experienced a wide range of settings prior to visiting school but the more dissimilar the setting, the more difficult it is for children to adjust. Barrett's study found that:

> Prior knowledge of the building, organisational patterns, people or activities gave both children and parents more confidence in that they were able to think about, anticipate, and therefore have some control over the new experience. (Barrett 1986: 96)

✎ **Activity 6.1**
In circle time, remind the children in your class about their first visit to school. Ask them what they wanted to see when they visited school for the first time. How would they improve the visit(s) for future children?

The way in which children and parents are introduced to their new environment is significant. What do people want to see? How much can they take in? How many times do they need to experience it before they know it? What do they need to become familiar with? Some parents find the library reassuring, others, the computer suite. It is not just the physical surroundings that they see when visiting a school but they also gain a feeling for the ethos of the school.

✎ **Activity 6.2**

Consider ways that you can create a physical and social climate of welcome and a positive atmosphere during visits. List the key principles that should guide the planning of pre-visits.

Giving information to parents

The initial meeting with parents is important. Some schools prefer to invite parents without their children the first time. If there is a large cohort, parents are more likely to be seen as a single group rather than treated as individuals. Smaller cohorts encourage a less formal atmosphere where parents and children can get to know one another, the teacher and the learning environment easily and, as a result, gain confidence in the system. Visits, with or without children, can take place at different times and have a range of formats:

- individually;
- a single afternoon or morning for either the whole group or small groups;
- a series of meetings that gradually build on previous knowledge and understanding;
- evening meeting for parents unable to attend a daytime session;
- meetings that inform parents about the curriculum.

Parents want to know pragmatic things about the school and what they have to do on the first day of school, such as who the teacher is, what is expected of them when they walk through the door, where their child hangs their coat, what happens if their child is ill, when the holiday dates are, where they wait at the end of the day. They also want practical advice on ways to support learning in preparation for school. During pre-start meetings information might be given about:

- a typical day in the Reception class;
- ways to become involved with the school;
- social events, e.g. parent-teacher association (PTA) functions;
- the curriculum, e.g. reading, numeracy;
- children's concert and sports day invitations;
- the school building;
- opportunities to borrow maths games, story sacks or library books;
- school systems for paying lunch money;
- where to buy the school uniform.

CASE STUDY 6.1

At one school a tour of the building, given by the head teacher for children and their parents, was used as a teaching time. This included:

- The toilets: She explained that urinals flushed automatically and that some children found this frightening. She demonstrated how to turn taps on, wash hands using liquid soap, dry hands using one paper towel and throw this in the bin.
- The secretary's office: She explained about knocking on the door, waiting for an answer. They met the secretary and were given information about what she does, e.g. photocopying.
- The head teacher's room: She showed them her desk and some fluffy toys.
- The hall: where some children were watching television.
- The staffroom: where some children were cooking. She explained that teachers need a rest sometimes and a space where they can meet.
- The library: She demonstrated how to select a book about dinosaurs, opened it and put it back in the right place.
- They walked back to the classroom and she congratulated children on walking quietly.

At another school the parents were taken on a tour without their children, and were invited to ask questions along the way. They saw:

- the playground;
- the Moderate Learning Difficulty unit;
- the computer suite;
- classrooms with closed doors;
- the open-plan section of the school;
- the cookery area;
- the reference library;
- the offices and staff room.

This might be done through:

- a video;
- speakers, e.g. brief presentations from the school secretary, someone from the governing body, the school nurse, a PTA representative, a parent from the previous year;
- a tour of the school, perhaps by older pupils;
- a photograph album;
- examples of work;
- displays of photographs and work on the walls.

Structures for parents to ask questions about things they do not understand should be in place. For example, give parents Post-its to write their questions on and stick them on a board; ask them to talk about their concerns in small groups and raise queries through a group leader. A shared understanding between parents and teachers may help children receive the same messages from each (Cousins 1990: 28).

For those parents who have had one child or more go through the process of starting school, it is more straightforward as they have a greater knowledge and understanding of the induction system itself and school generally. However, schools and the curriculum are changing, so these parents need to be encouraged to attend induction meetings and given the same opportunities as new parents.

Virtual visits

Visits can be assisted by technology. In adapting systems to the needs of children and their parents, this might mean using email as a home–school link before the start of, and during, transition, to contribute to an understanding of school. The use of the school web site or an interactive CD-ROM could include a tour of school where children can experience their classroom, 'meet' their teacher and 'try it on for size' before they arrive. This would avoid large groups on visits, when children may get upset, and give an insight into classroom life for those parents unable to make any real visits.

Meeting people

Visits to school are not just about getting to know the school building but also about meeting the people. Parents and children want to know who the teacher is and what he or she looks like. Parents want reassurances about the staff who will be with their children and to meet other parents. The children need to meet their teacher and other children.

The Reception class teacher is a key figure in the anticipation of school. Children and parents want to know the name of the teacher, meet and get to know him or her at an early stage in the induction process. Children are confused if the person who works with them during pre-entry visits is not their teacher when they begin school. Parents consider the personality and experience of the first teacher as significant factors in whether or not their child will learn well and be happy at school. Cleave and Brown (1991: 197) found that 'particular skills and experiences were required' in the first teacher.

Bronfenbrenner (1979) suggests that the developmental potential of a setting is enhanced if the child's initial transition into that setting is in the company of one or more people from a previous setting who can make the link between the two. For example, the child's mother serves as a source of security, provides a role model of social interaction and is of significance for the way in which the child is able to function in the new setting, if she accompanies the child on the first visit and especially if she converses with the teacher.

Teachers can help children get to know one another by:

- pairing children with more experienced peers if there are older children in the class;
- using children's names (some teachers make name labels for children when they first start);
- introducing children to one another;
- circle time where discussion takes place about feelings.

Parents too need opportunities to meet one another. Some schools have a parents' room where they can meet together and have refreshments, perhaps organised by the PTA or 'established' parents.

Gaining an understanding of the nature of school

What is it that schools are hoping for when children visit the classroom? Is it to give them an idea about the excitement of learning? Is it to give them an understanding of what it means to be at school? What activities are going to be provided? Are they similar to those experienced at preschool which they can do and which will give children confidence? Do activities convey that school might be different? Are they directed activities which help the teacher make simple assessments of cognitive development?

During the pre-entry visits to school, children are often presented with activities such as role-play, drawing, painting and building with construction toys to give them a 'taste' of school. Although they are likely to come across these when they start, they will also have a much broader curriculum and therefore may gain the wrong impression of school at this juncture. The visits do not necessarily help children to understand the nature of school because they do not experience the curriculum, the length of the day or their peer group. They may also think that school education is normally part-time if they have several short visits that they view as 'going to school'. Many children think that they have 'started school' after a first visit.

What is the role of the teacher during visits? Is it to assess social ability, encourage children to make friends, give children a fun time or a preparation for new challenges and a new culture? Bruner (1996a) highlights the use of story to resolve the unexpected for children and as a vehicle for meaning making. One way of helping children to understand the way in which classrooms function is through stories about school that link past and present experiences and that give an indication of school and its culture. Cultural exchange is a two-way process. If children tell stories of themselves, teachers might also get an insight into the children's culture and their thinking.

How are children helped to cope with the emotional and social challenges they meet? One approach may be that the induction visits are more like a school day in content and in the people whom children meet. Another may be that induction visits are timed as near to the start of school as possible because breaks cause discontinuity. Schools might help children to gain a feel of the length of a school day by gradually increasing the length of the visits to include aspects such as playtime, lunch-time and assembly.

✎ Activity 6.3

Consider your own setting. Is there an opportunity for children to spend time in their new classroom before admission? What happens during these visits that helps children understand school practices and routines? What is the purpose of the activities on offer to children?

- Outline a programme that indicates what the visit(s) will cover and who will be involved. This might include planning for support staff and using some of the time to meet with parents individually.
- Will children be introduced to playtime, lunch-time and assembly during the visits? These can be distressing times. What can you do to help children?

Information sharing

Induction is not necessarily a one-way process but an opportunity for a two-way flow of information. Parents and teachers should have a working knowledge of each other if children are to benefit fully. Parents know when their 'children feel pleased with themselves, when they are confident or fearful and when they are truly interested' (Dowling 2000: 133). At the start of school most parents want to share this vast knowledge and understanding about their child's attributes with the teacher in a way that is easy for them, while giving relevant information to the teacher. If teachers are to build on this, then working in partnership with parents, getting to know each family and viewing parents as supporters of learning, might give continuity to children's education.

Teachers also want information about children's ability to learn. When children start school they are at different developmental stages and their learning experiences vary widely. With the introduction of baseline assessment (QCA 1998), primary schools now have a statutory duty to assess children in the Reception year. If teachers have little in the way of information about the children before they begin, the start of school may be a time of curriculum discontinuity. The Select Committee (House of Commons 2001) recommends a developmental profile at entry to school that includes parents' contributions. If teachers know about children's previous experiences and their stage of development, they are more likely to achieve a better match of activities to learning ability and provide appropriate progression in learning (Emery 1993: 8). Many schools already adopt pre-entry profiles that involve parents and children sharing information with teachers. However, pre-entry profiles need to be explained clearly if parents are to help the school identify what their children have learnt and how they learnt it. They can be used to help parents to see how their children approach an activity and help teachers to know the ways children respond and what they need to learn next.

CASE STUDY 6.2

In my study of 50 parents, 76 per cent were expecting to complete some form of pre-entry profile and thought that it might be useful as they might find out their child's capabilities. This has implications for the content of the profile if it is to solve such queries. Parents felt that the school and parents should work together in partnership on the profiles. However, some were unsure as to their benefit and a sizeable minority thought that such profiles were a measurement of the quality of their parenting. They felt that completing pre-entry booklets about colour and shape with their child was testing *them* rather than helping the teacher find out about their child's achievement. Some parents questioned whether they were answered honestly, some experienced guilt feelings if they were not completed, some perceived that it was they who were being put under scrutiny and others thought that teachers would ignore the profiles altogether.

(Fabian 1998)

✎ Activity 6.4

Consider ways that you can gain information about individual children before they come to school. What is it that you need to know? How will you record and use the information? Some schools have information sheets such as the following.

BEFORE I COME TO SCHOOL

All About Me

(Photograph and date)

My name is:

My birthday is on:

My favourite story is:

My favourite toy is:

Things that frighten me are:

At school I am looking forward to:

This is a drawing of where I live and my family:

These people will collect me from school:

_____

Mum or Dad,
Please add a comment about any things that you feel may help us with your child.

_____

Other schools have drawings of activities that children colour in when they have achieved them.

Others ask for information about understanding in each area of learning.

CHAPTER 7

The first day at school

Key issues
- What admission procedures take place at the start of school?
- What makes an effective learning environment for children starting school?
- How are children and parents helped to deal with the initial separation?
- How can schools support parents through their own transition as their children start school?

Admission procedures

Procedures for allocating children to a class or teacher will depend on numbers of pupils in the school overall and the number of classes that children are to enter. The organisation of classes will affect placements, with some children entering a class where there is already an established group of older pupils. This allows a smaller number of new children to enter the class, giving the teacher time to focus on individuals, and older children in the class the opportunity to act as role models. A mixed-aged class can also mean a wider differentiation in levels of achievement. If children are to be divided between a number of classes, friendship groups need to be taken into account and parents' wishes concerning the placement of twins. In other situations the entire class will comprise a group of children who start school together, with up to 30 pupils in the class.

Even for those children who have been in full-time preschool education, a day can seem a long time and five full days can be exhausting. Part-time or staggered entry policies enable a gradual introduction to school, time for children to become familiar with routines and expectations and time for adults to give their attention to individual children's needs. However, this flexibility can cause disruption for some children and requires good organisational skills on the part of the teacher. Children might:

- start with the rest of the school on the first day of term;
- arrive later than the others on the first day;
- have a staggered start with individuals starting at intervals throughout the day;
- be admitted over two days;
- begin in groups for a day each, over two or three days, with all the children attending on the fourth day;
- have staggered arrival and departure times over a number of days, either singly or in groups;
- attend for half-days for the first few days or weeks;
- be admitted in groups every third day over a two-week period.

The adopted system could be different for children starting later in the year.

Children's differences need to be acknowledged beyond the first week. For example, some schools have special lunch-time arrangements for the first half of term with children going home for lunch or having lunch earlier than the rest of the school, or staff sitting with the children at lunch-time. Schools offering this type of flexibility recognise children as individuals who are becoming more independent but who need security and adult support (Cleave and Brown 1991).

Part-time attendance has evolved in some schools in response to school organisation and to meet individual needs (Cleave and Brown 1991). Many schools might have part-time pupils in the Reception class:

- until they are of statutory school age;
- for two or three weeks at the beginning of term, usually with the youngest children attending in the afternoon;
- for the first half term;
- based on negotiation between parents and teachers, depending on how well the child settles into school.

One circumstance of the private and public partnership is that some children may have been attending a nursery full-time but then only be offered a part-time place in school. This may result in some parents not accepting the Reception place for their child or delaying the start.

✎ **Activity 7.1**

Look at your admission procedures. Would a staggered entry alleviate the difficulties of acclimatising large numbers of pupils all at the same time? Could this be done in a way to advantage the summer-born children?

Preparing the learning environment

Classrooms reflect the philosophy of the teacher but there is sometimes a danger of an inflexible programme that treats children as raw material to be shaped into 'school children'. Are schools places that bring about conformity or places where children participate, develop, discover and learn how to co-operate with one another? An environment in which children feel confident and secure requires sensitivity and awareness in its organisation of resources, space, display areas and furniture.

If children are to become independent they must learn to make choices and find resources for themselves without having to refer to adults (Dowling 2000: 41). Therefore, the classroom needs to be organised to promote independence, self-reliance and decision-making skills. This has implications not only for organising the room logically in designated areas of learning and having equipment clearly labelled and easily accessible, but also for showing the children what is available, where resources are kept and the way in which they are to be maintained.

Although starting school may be seen as an exciting step, excitement can easily turn to anxiety if not supported. To ease the initial separation from parents, the Reception class teacher can prepare the classroom by including:

- a display of pictures and drawings that the children made in preschool;
- a labelled coat peg for each child. Parents could be asked to provide a photo-graph, or a photograph taken during visits could be put next to the coat peg with the child's name to make it meaningful;
- a trolley or box for storing lunch boxes;
- a labelled drawer for belongings.

The environment and routines need to be planned to give children a sense of belonging, and structured to give children ownership and a feeling that they contribute to the class. School routines are usually determined by the school timetable with fixed times such as assembly, lunch, play and hall times where children have to cope with large groups and spaces, often some distance away from their classroom. However, a flexible and sensitive approach to appropriate routines can alleviate potential difficulties. For example, the Reception class might have a different break time from the rest of the school (although some will miss older siblings), make visits to the assembly hall to see what it looks like prior to assembly, and start lunch earlier than the rest of the school to allow longer to choose and to eat their food. This will give children time to assimilate their surroundings.

The first teacher

Evidence indicates that a positive start to school not only gives an initial boost to children's education but also provides them with an advantage throughout their schooling (Tizard *et al.* 1988; Pascal 1990). Many factors play a critical part in determining the progress children make in their first year of school but research suggests that the first teacher is very important to children (Hennessy 1998). The qualities of the Reception class teacher and the way he or she interacts with children have a significant impact not only on a child's development, but also on the way they settle in and adjust to school. Furthermore, the impact of the first teacher seems to last beyond the years spent with the child (Pedersen *et al.* 1978).

The role of the Reception class teacher is demanding and complex. Dowling (1995: 9) identified several key aspects of the role over and above those for teachers of older pupils. These are summarised here:

- bringing together a group from diverse backgrounds and widely different educational experience who have no shared history;
- assisting children to become pupils and learn as a group;
- establishing prior learning and taking individuals forward from that point;
- ensuring continuity of the curriculum from preschool;
- planning that provides for teacher-responsive and teacher-directed activities;
- working in close partnership with parents to share the progress of pupils whose learning is often intangible;
- articulating the philosophy of an early years education to those who may be more conversant with a subject-focused curriculum;
- becoming an educational ambassador to parents to promote the child's best chances of success.

The strangeness of the new school situation for the entrant can be alleviated by the warmth and skill of an experienced Reception class teacher (Barrett 1986). If children are going to settle in to their new environment quickly then a secure attachment to the teacher and maintaining high levels of self-esteem are important to help them respond positively to the social and emotional climate of the setting. Teachers who are open and responsive to children's and parents' needs help promote this. Certain styles of teacher behaviour such as genuineness, acceptance and empathy have been found to be positively related to increased pupil learning (Rogers 1983), therefore the teacher's attitude plays an important part in introducing children to a new setting and in establishing routines and a positive classroom ethos.

The feedback that adults give the children is crucial for their adjustment to school. According to Gipps *et al.* (1996) feedback serves three functions:

- as part of the socialisation process;
- to encourage and motivate children;
- to identify aspects of attainment.

A study by Burrell and Bubb (2000) found that effective feedback could be a powerful strategy in combating low self-esteem as it can assist in the promotion of positive attitudes to learning in all children and give them confidence in their ability to be successful learners from an early age.

The first day

What happens when the children arrive for their first day at school? They will probably have met their teacher and seen their classroom on their visits, but directions to the classroom and photographs of staff give a welcoming atmosphere. Name labels for the teacher and classroom assistant(s) remind parents of personnel. Greeting the children by name and giving them a name label helps identification and makes them feel welcome.

Cleave *et al.* (1982) state that the key to the start of school 'seems to lie in avoiding the shock of anything sudden in the way of sights, sounds or experiences, and in introducing everything gradually in an atmosphere of unhurried calm' (Cleave *et al.* 1982: 121). This means giving children time:

- to find their coat peg, and staff to point out their name and the picture next to it;
- to say goodbye to their parent(s);
- to be reminded about the location of toilets and washbasins;
- to be introduced to each other through 'getting to know you' activities, and supported by staff using children's names whenever possible;
- to talk through the routine of the day and for staff to remind children throughout the day of where they are up to.

Having prepared the environment, children need to be shown what is there, and trained and trusted to use it. This does not happen in one day. When they first arrive they need to be shown what is available to them, understand the sort of activities that take place and how to return materials after they have finished with them. Many will have had experience of finding resources and tidying away afterwards at preschool but they will still need plenty of time to do this when they start school before they become knowledgeable about where things belong and the way that they are expected to behave with them.

In mixed-age classes it is sometimes helpful to pair a new child with an older child. Although it is difficult to match kindred spirits, pairing can be reassuring for the new child and give the older child confidence, too. However, the older child needs to know the routines, otherwise they can mislead unintentionally. Further difficulties are that they can become bossy, the novelty can wear off quickly or they would prefer to be with their own friends. Some form of mentor training may make them more effective in this role.

Helping children and parents to say goodbye

There are considerable challenges for children, parents and practitioners during the early days of school. Some children become distressed on their first day at school and find it difficult to make the separation from their parents or carer. They might be unsure about being left 'on their own', shy about large groups or strange people, or anxious that their parent might not return. Some children have to deal with an anxious parent and may worry how their parent(s) will cope without them (Waksler 1996: 145). Some self-reliant children would prefer to go into school by themselves as they see school as their world and not for their parents.

Some families make the first day of school into a big event, with grandparents sending cards and parents taking photographs. Some children will leave their parents easily and enjoy the ritual of finding their coat peg, hanging up their coat and going into the classroom. Even though children are excited about school and have been looking forward to it, the reality on the day might be different for others. The activity of the classroom, the amount of children or choice might be overwhelming in its enormity. The anxiety of separating shows itself in different ways. Some children will go straight in and not look back, some children will be tearful and cling to their parent. Any attempts for the parent to leave are then often greeted with loud howls and an attempt to pull them back. Many children will want an extra hug or kiss, others might burst into tears as their parent leaves. Parents see their role as one of providing support and security at this time (Dalli 1999), but if the parent responds to anxiety with anxiety this can make the situation worse and even turn it into a daily drama. Other children may show their anxiety by sitting passively on their own.

Anxiety can become contagious and influence other children in the class. It is a reasonable response to a difficult or threatening situation but it has to be managed. However, children need to be 'allowed' to get upset or angry at times. Teachers are concerned to provide a positive start and generate a calm ethos, but this can be undermined when faced with a situation where a child and parent find it difficult to part. An ability to stay calm and empathise with the situation will help. The quiet children will also need comforting. Children need reassurance and an explanation that their parent will return. Distracting and involving the child in an activity either on his or her own or with others can turn attention away from the tension generated by the separation. Children might already know some of the others in the class and be guided towards them. Teachers and classroom assistants in a child-ready school will have a good knowledge of individual children before they begin, including children's friends, and this helps to determine children's starting point so they experience themselves as being competent and active individuals from the beginning of their school career.

> ✎ **Activity 7.2**
> What helps and what hinders on the first day of school? Start by thinking of an example when you have been the new person somewhere. How did you feel? What would you have liked to have had happen that would have helped you settle in to the situation? What hindered you from feeling comfortable and competent in the situation? Transfer this to the child's perspective on their first day at school. How do you think they could be helped? Support is also needed for those children who appear confident or to have settled, but are bottling it all up until they arrive home.

Parents, too, experience this emotional turmoil. They need reassurance that their child is in capable hands, that no harm will come to them and that they will be happy. Their behaviour is transmitted to their child, making a difference to their child's emotional state and the way their child reacts, thus influencing the starting point of their child's school experience.

> The way the parent feels about sending the child to school will have a profound effect on the way the child adjusts. If she feels reluctant, unsure or overanxious, she hinders his ability to meet the new situation and grow more independent. (Read and Patterson 1976: 138)

Children who feel confident in themselves and their own learning ability have a head start in learning. If parents are encouraged to leave quickly and let the teacher take responsibility, they not only indicate that they trust the teacher but also help the child to develop that trust (Dalli 1999: 61).

Strategies for helping parents separate from their child on the first day include:

- giving reassurance;
- not prolonging the moment of separation;
- suggesting that they arrive with another new family. This will give support for the children and parents;

- if the separation was tearful, encouraging parents to phone later to check that their child has settled. Tell the parent what the child has been doing and what they are doing at that moment rather than give bland reassurances;
- taking a photo of children on the first day of school and displaying it at the end of the day; this will inform parents about their children's activities during the day.

Parents and educators are working together to support children's learning and develop children's confidence in what they can do. Arrival and departure times are a time when parents can be involved, for example, having a signing-in procedure that encourages a routine and encourages parents to support the daily transition.

Parents' transition

Children's start at school is loaded with emotional uncertainty for parents and makes an impact on their well-being due to feelings such as 'losing' their child and having to learn how to cope without them (Elfer 1997). For some there are feelings of jealousy, for others concerns about safety and care or about the nature of the partnership with school and the information exchange systems. Some are delighted to have more personal time. The start of school may be the first contact that parents have had with the school system since being a pupil themselves, which may bring associated feelings (Waterland 1994). This then is also a transition for parents full of mixed emotions such as anxiety, pride, expectations and hope. Support networks and coping strategies may also be needed for parents.

When their child starts school, many parents often plan for the 'loss' of their child by organising a busy schedule of events for themselves during the first few weeks of term, for example by attending courses or returning to employment. Those with younger children expect to be able to spend more time with them; those without younger children expect to feel empty and many would appreciate a support group for parents of the last child (Fabian 1996).

One way to support parents through their own transition might be to include them more fully by giving them an induction into the nature of learning and social practices at school and the possible levels of their involvement. This might be through:

- parent conferences where they can begin to evolve the nature of the partnership with school;
- a mentoring system for new parents by parents of children who began school the previous year. This requires systems to be in place for effective mentoring to support those who are doing the mentoring;

• creating a forum for parents to share ideas and problems, often through consideration of home–school partnership issues.

Parents might then be able to take a greater role in preparing their children for school and develop strategies as a team to cope with the start of school. However, it must be remembered that not all parents want, or are able, to be involved with school.

PART 3

Preschools, Schools and Families Working Together

CHAPTER 8

Liaison between settings

Key issues
- How can preschool settings help in the transition to Key Stage 1?
- How can schools develop partnerships with their local preschool services?

Traditionally preschool settings and schools have been separate institutions with two different, and often contradictory, cultures and ideological goals. They have developed their own organisational systems independently of one another but, to make the transfer for children as advantageous as possible, they need to collaborate. Just as there is a need to create a bridge between preschool and school, there is also a need for good contacts with other agencies to address the needs of particular children. Part of this communication should consider how the transition is presented to parents, as preschool is often viewed as helping children with social integration whereas entry to school is viewed as a life event. It is helpful if staff can articulate any differences in teaching approaches between preschool and school to parents. Another essential part of the transition is helping children to understand the differences that they may come across.

Preschool preparations

One widespread activity of early childhood settings is preparing children for compulsory schooling and starting school 'ready to learn'. However, this notion of school readiness can be problematic because learning is then seen as preparing children for the future rather than for helping them function well in the present. Holliday (2001) and Dahlberg *et al*. (1999) argue that the view that preschool contributes to children being ready to learn by the time they start school, produces a picture of a child in need of preparation before they can be expected to learn, rather than one whose learning is in a child-responsive system that is part of a continuous process of lifelong learning. If the ethos of school is so alien to four- and five-year-olds that they need to be prepared for it then, they suggest, it is the formal nature of school that needs changing. The issue, therefore, is whether the school is prepared for the variety of settings that children will come from and able to help children continue learning.

Rather than learning in readiness, an understanding of each other's settings would be more beneficial. This might promote a seamless pathway rather than disconnected thinking. It could start by recognising and anticipating some of the differences between preschool and school while continuing with familiar routines. The Early Learning Goals (QCA 1999) and curriculum guidance on the Foundation Stage (QCA 2000) enable the curriculum to be continuous but in other areas the following differences can often exist:

- Many children will have attended a preschool setting with children of their own age, but they might not have had the opportunity of relating to older children.
- There may be larger numbers of pupils in school. For those who have attended a small preschool group or none at all, they will now have to co-operate with larger numbers and a wide range of age groups. This is especially the case in a small school where several age groups are in one class. In addition, a new pupil moves from being the oldest child in preschool to the youngest child in school (Woolfson 1993: 13). Some children, therefore, do not feel they succeed as well as previously because they are not always the first or 'the best'. With greater numbers there often comes greater competition.
- At home some children may have an adult's undivided attention or share it with one or two siblings. Children are likely to have different staffing ratios at school and have fewer staff to interact with than at their preschool setting. This might mean less interaction with adults than previously. This increase in pupil–teacher ratios leads to the expectation from staff that children will do more for themselves (Curtis 1986: 153).
- Each child has more peer group relationships to enjoy than in the preschool stage (Cleave and Brown 1991: 13).
- At school pupils are often expected to work independently and find solutions on their own.
- School is often in a larger building. Those children who attend preschools usually do so in small self-contained buildings used only by children who are close to each other in age (Woolfson 1993: 35). The first class of school, on the other hand, is usually part of a larger infant department, and often an even larger primary school. Even in those schools where a nursery class is part of the school, it is likely to be a self-contained unit with few opportunities to explore the rest of the school (Curtis 1986).

- The vocabulary of the preschool will be extended and there might be unfamiliar words or words used in a different way at school.

Some preschools prepare children for school by giving them worksheets and formal lessons. However, 'well-meaning educators can waste time and insult the intellect of young children by requiring them to do things that they will need to do "when they go to school"' (Nutbrown 1994: 126). Dahlberg and Asen (1994), Sharp (1998) and the Department of Education Northern Ireland (2000) found that those preschool programmes relying on a more holistic and dynamic notion of childhood seem to be more successful in helping children towards independence than those programmes intent upon acquiring academic skills. Rather than giving children worksheets and introducing them to formal work in preschool, schools might be better to encourage preschools to prepare children by developing their self-confidence, listening skills, curiosity, cooperation, sociability and independence (Woolfson 1999). Personal, rather than intellectual, ability is the success to giving children the best start to school. Social confidence and a sense of success play an important part in giving children self-esteem which will, in turn, help children to approach the start of school in a positive way (Illsley Clarke 1997). This supports Goleman's notion that by developing early emotional literacy children's academic achievement is improved (Goleman 1996).

Some preschools use the notion of school as a threat when a child misbehaves. By avoiding negative associations with school, preschools can also help to develop a positive attitude to school.

Developing relationships with preschool

Increasingly preschools and schools see a need to work together to prepare children for school. Sometimes preschools 'feed' a number of schools and are having to learn about a number of different systems; in other cases, the preschool is on site and the Reception and preschool teachers rotate their teaching roles. This is not to say that one is easier than the other, although pre-admission visits are usually easier to arrange if the preschool links are with one school and if good liaison has been established.

Activities that involve children to begin the process of bridging the gap to school include:

- pupils from the school to visit the preschool setting and talk about school;
- mentoring 'partners' from the Reception year to visit preschool;
- reception pupils emailing preschool children to inform them about school, possibly through photographs taken with a digital camera;
- visits from a small group of older children who can become 'known persons'

CASE STUDY 8.1

This is an extract from a conversation that I had with a preschool leader about the way she prepared children for school:

> We try to make them more independent as such by encouraging them to go to the toilet by themselves, and making them aware of personal hygiene. They put aprons on and hang their coats up on the hook. We won't put their shoes and socks on for them, unless they try for themselves first.
>
> We talk about going to school but I can't really tell them much because I don't know. They pick things up and we look at books about starting school. The ones with older brothers and sisters tell the others about it.
>
> We don't change the day for the older ones. We hope the things we do, like cutting and construction, are preparing them for school. I'd like school to come and see what we're doing more.

This preschool resisted the temptation to have a formal training programme in the last few months before children started school. Instead, they continued with their normal Foundation Stage curriculum and helped children to practise social skills through:

- separating from their parent(s) with confidence;
- getting dressed independently;
- being able to use the toilet;
- turn-taking;
- listening to other children;
- working with other children in pairs and small groups;
- being able to introduce themselves to others;
- knowing about foods, and eating with a knife and fork;
- responding to questions from adults;
- talking about school, their expectations and encouraging them to ask questions.

to go to when the new intake starts. This strategy might help to overcome any fear of big children;
- arranging visits to the infant school so children can see the school and begin to familiarise themselves with the environment. These visits could have a particular focus, for example story time. More questions will probably ensue from visits;
- visits to school for selected assemblies, or a concert;
- visits to school in small groups, with the teacher answering questions previously collated from the whole group;
- playpacks shared between school and preschool during the transition.

Just as the preschool's idea of school procedures is vague (see Case study 8.1), very often the school's knowledge of preschool is equally vague. There is a need to develop an understanding of the philosophy and procedures by exchanging information. In the next case study, the preschool leader explains the connections with the feeder schools.

CASE STUDY 8.2

The children go to two schools when they leave playgroup. Most want to go across the road. The teachers come to see the children. We hadn't seen anyone for a long time from down the other end but the new morning member of staff has a child there so the teacher came up to see us. We'd like to see the children, the ones who went last time, but it's too much to expect. When the teacher comes, we introduce her to the children who are going to school. She likes to read them a story and play with them in the paint and playdough. It's very informal. Our children are invited to school to visit but it varies each term how many times they go. The parents take them in the afternoon. We'd like to see them visiting school more often but the school decides.

Practitioners working together to share information as children move from one stage to another reduces disruption in children's lives. In planning a coordinated transition programme, it is important to consider continuity of expectations and peers:

- arrange meetings to discuss the programme, children's continuity and focus for visits;
- release time for adult visits;
- ask preschool staff to make a list of queries that children have about school;
- share videos of school activities;
- keep in contact throughout the year as well as having ongoing communication between staff before the move;
- consider the format of record keeping from nursery;
- exchange roles for a day.

It is useful to have a meeting between preschool and school staff shortly after children have started, to provide the opportunity for staff to ask questions and share information, particularly with regard to behaviour. Cleave and Brown (1991) cite one school where the nursery children started their term a week later than the Reception class to enable nursery staff to spend the first week of term with the new entrants in the Reception class.

Induction or curriculum continuity might include:

- joint in-service training of staff;
- exchange of newsletters and information;
- planning the transition programme jointly.

Joint advice from preschool and school can be given to parents while the children are still at the preschool setting to reassure parents who may be anxious about their child's transition.

> ✎ **Activity 8.1**
>
> Make a book about life in the Reception class to show to the preschool children to help them develop an understanding of school culture and minimise their anxieties. This can include photos and captions about the adults, areas of the classroom, cloakroom and activities that take place.

CHAPTER 9

Early links between home and school

Key issues
- Does home visiting bridge the gap between home and school?
- How can schools help parents to help their children before they start school?
- What is the child's view of partnership?
- What are home–school agreements?

There has been growing recognition of the primacy of parents as the first educators of young children through reports by Plowden (DES 1967), Taylor (DES 1977), Rumbold (DES 1990) and Ball (1994), and of the parent as the one constant element in the child's experience during the transition process (Miller 1994; DES 1990). It is also recognised that it is 'the quality of involvement or partnership between parents and educators which is likely to determine effectiveness of continuity' (DES 1990 para. 106). This, therefore, is a strong case for ensuring that parents are an integral part of the transition process and that parents and teachers establish an effective collaboration in the early stages of transition in order to understand each other's worlds. Without this sharing of dialogue the different views of teachers and parents about the education process may well hinder the child's transition. A shared understanding may help to avoid assumptions made on both sides.

If teachers are to develop some understanding about each family's goals and needs, then they must really get to know each family and view parents as learners about school (Barbour 1995). Parents generally wish to make contributions to their children's education (Wolfendale 1989), and teachers need to respect and value the knowledge, expertise and experience that parents bring. However, family patterns are changing and schools are having to cater for an ever-diversifying range of family structures and parenting strategies. The perception of parents as partners rests on the assumption that teachers and parents are jointly and equally engaged in educating children and that both partners in this enterprise have something to offer (Hughes *et al.* 1994). In some families, however, there is no single main adult contact between home and school, or that contact may not be the child's parent (Hallgarten 2000).

When does partnership begin? Some parents have begun a partnership with school because of an older sibling but, 'if positive relationships are to be established between parent and school, they must be begun before the child starts' (Cleave *et al.* 1982: 103). This means for each new child in a family. Fieldhouse (1988) suggests that schools make contact with parents as early as possible and 'as much as a year or at least two terms prior to admission' to allow for both formal and informal opportunities to be offered. Policies that encourage early parental involvement in pupils' learning and in school life will contribute to the general raising of individual and school achievement (Hallgarten 2000). Parents also benefit from early involvement and gain increased confidence in themselves as educators of their children and in relating to professionals (Maclachlan 1995).

Home visits

Plowden suggests that one way of beginning to work with parents 'would be for teachers to ask parents if they would be willing to be visited at home, and if they were, to do so' (DES 1967 para. 113).

As part of the school's wider induction programme, home visiting may have a range of benefits. It provides an opportunity not only for the child to get to know the teacher in a familiar environment where they may feel more confident, but also for parents to talk about their concerns and wishes and to give valuable information about the nature of their child (Stelling and Fabian 1996). Having an information booklet about school and the induction programme, and an opportunity to contribute to their child's initial assessment, reassures parents, assists in raising their self-esteem and encourages them to be involved in their child's education. Furthermore, they are more likely 'to both understand and support the school system' (Curtis 1986: 160). Home visiting helps teachers gain knowledge about children's previous learning. It can aid appreciation of diversity and different cultural expectations, thus helping teachers recognise differences as well as common interests of families and become more aware of parenting behaviours that might conflict with their expectations. The present changing context of the family probably results in the need for increasing support and access to advice, which home visits might be able to provide.

While the rewards of closer working relationships between parents and teachers are considerable, there are no easy solutions to putting them into practice. Bastiani (1993) warns that teacher opinion is deeply divided on home visiting and what works in one school may not work in another. Parents will vary in their acceptance and application of any advice that is given, as will teachers in their ability to communicate ideas and use the information they gain from parents. Home visiting is a skilled and difficult task which may require training. Many teachers visit with a classroom assistant to ensure practitioners' personal safety. It might put pressure on some families (Cohen 1988), although for many families the visit will be seen as an important social occasion. An interpreter might be necessary on visits to families for whom English is an additional language. Parents will want to know about the procedures and approach to learning and have the opportunity to voice any concerns about their child. Equally, staff will want to find out about how the child responds to change and challenge. Often children want to show their new teacher a favourite toy, their bedroom or pet. This gives a valuable opportunity for the child to take the lead in the interaction, but on the other hand, they might be shy and have difficulty in communicating.

There has been little research into children's reactions to home visits but work done by Cousins (1990) indicates that they value the opportunity for a personal link. Many children, however, want to keep home and school separate and do not want teachers to transgress the boundaries. Indeed, once having started at school, children see 'assessments of them were for the school's and their parents' benefit, not for themselves' (Black 1998: 129).

✎ **Activity 9.1**

What do you see as the benefits and costs of developing home visiting as part of the induction policy in your school? Look at it from the perspective of the staff, parents and children.

If you decide to have home visiting as part of a wider induction programme, what is its purpose? What will take place during the visit? How long will it last? What will you take? Some teachers take along a welcome pack that contains paper, crayons and a storybook for the child; literature for the parents or a video of life at school. How will you record the visit?

Supporting early learning

Children begin school with a variety of experiences and different levels of intellectual development and social competence. These differences 'reinforce the importance of close cooperation with parents in making the transition from home to school and helping the children to cope with the demands of a busy school day' (NCC 1989: 18). The starting point for this close cooperation in many schools is a pre-entry visit, but many parents would welcome information on helping their child and opportunities, long before the first visit, to have contact with the school and to gain information and direction on preparing their children for formal learning (Fabian 1998). Certainly, parents have high expectations of the partnership with school, although they do not always know what form it will take or who manages it. Schools need to take advantage of this enthusiasm from parents before children start school to create a two-way process that leads to an integrated experience for the child.

CASE STUDY 9.1

In this extract we see Lorraine reflecting on the support that she'd like in order to help Stacey learn.

From: <Lorraine@talk.com>
To: <Debbie@ezyfriend.net>
Subject: Learning at home
Date: June

Dear Debbie,
   The tour of the school gave me a feel of the place but not about what goes on in a class. What I'd like to know is how Stacey compares to the norm. I've steered clear of doing too much with her before she starts in case she has to redo it. I think I've been teaching her the alphabet and reading the wrong way. I want to get it right but I feel as if I'm working in the dark. I would've liked to have been given some guidelines so I'm not clashing with the school.
   I don't know what they'll suggest once she starts. I expect I'll have to practise words and reading with her and writing exercises, but nothing major because she'll be too tired at the end of the day. If I know what they're doing I can do things at home. Perhaps they'll put up a notice telling us what topic they're doing, but really what I'll want to know is how she's getting on and the things she needs pulling up on. I want to be kept informed and told the truth. It'll be good for Stacey if she knows that I'm in contact with the school.
   It's difficult because the teacher is taking her over. She'll suddenly have someone else and she might not want to tell me anything any more. I think I'll try and get involved and join the PTA and go on trips and things so I'll know what's going on.
   I'm sorry to trouble you with all my worries. I expect you went through all this with James so it won't be so bad this time . . .

Lorraine

(Adapted from Fabian 1998)

This lack of knowledge at pre-entry can contrast with information overload during induction. No one explicitly told parents in the above case study what the partnership might look like, although at the induction talk the head teacher said: 'You have a role to play in your child's education. You're a partner and we encourage you to take part.' Sharing of information about expectations of the partnership itself, prior to the start of school, might clarify and guide its development.

Robson (1996) suggests that within the home–school partnership there are unidirectional relationships involving information, contact and involvement, and reciprocal ones that include collaboration and partnership. Induction to school is not a one-way process, in which the child and his or her family adjust to school, but a complementary one where there are opportunities for each party to influence the other. Bastiani states 'parents and teachers are both educational influences, each with their own special contributions to make' (Bastiani 1995: 7). This contribution may not necessarily be in equal parts as there will be an element of give and take by all concerned. Neither can it be assumed that all parents want a close partnership with school, as their amount of involvement will vary according to their circumstances and wishes. The effectiveness of the partnership is most likely to be determined by its perceived quality.

Parental support at home

Parents are interested in their own children's education and view part of their role as parents as giving support to learning at home (Bastiani 1995).

> Children's experiences at home are highly significant to achievement. Parents significantly influence their children's learning. (SCAA 1996: 7)

The potential of all homes, even those in extreme poverty, as contexts for learning is now recognised. Indeed, Wells (1986) and Tizard and Hughes (1984) have demonstrated how families can provide a rich learning environment for their children. Parental participation programmes such as the Headstart programme (Berrueta-Clement *et al.* 1984) have made it clear that the long-term effects of children's development and success are a result of early parent–child interaction, the active participation of parents in their children's learning process and the expectations they have of their children (Sylva and Moss 1992). Home learning may be deliberate or unintentional, it may be enlightened or misinformed, but it is powerful, complex and contextualised.

Nutbrown (1994: 130–31) found parents' views of the part they played in their child's learning fell into three categories:

- parents who did not recognise the things they did as helping their children to learn;
- parents who felt that they helped 'informally' at home;
- parents who felt they did a lot to help their children to learn but felt that the benefits of nursery education enhanced what they could do.

Not only do parents need mechanisms to share their child's previous learning with teachers, but teachers, too, need ways to give parents knowledge about ways in which children learn and ways in which they can make an informed contribution to their child's learning. Nutbrown notes that:

> Parents who are informed in some way about the ways in which children learn, think about and represent their thoughts through talk, drawing and action are in a better position to support the continuity and progression of their children's learning and development between home and nursery, school or other group setting. (Nutbrown 1994: 131–2)

Parents cannot be expected to support learning if they do not know about or understand the strategies available. If schools are to provide information to increase parental involvement in their child's education, activities will 'need to be responsive to the language and culture of the family and be tailored to meet specific needs of teen parents, single parents, working parents, blended families, and families with special service needs' (Lombardi 1992). A workshop approach conducted by Vopat (1994: 14) comprised six two-hour workshops which included a mix of experiential activities, guest presentations, journal writing, shared books and specific attention to activities that parents could do at home to support their children's learning.

If education is to be seen as a continuum, the working links made with parents before their child starts school should ideally be sustained through each transition. By not encouraging an early partnership between home and school, opportunities may be missed for developing children's early stages of lifelong learning.

✎ Activity 9.2

Make a list of what you think parents want to know about learning at school and ways to help parents understand the learning that takes place in the home and in daily family life. How will you find out what they want? How can you support them in helping their child to learn before the start of school? Some schools have a toy library, maths pack or story sack lending, or a book shop that children and parents have access to before their child begins school.

How can you help parents understand about specific subject areas? Some schools have workshops for parents.

Home–school agreements

One method of promoting a robust and dynamic relationship between home and school is through home–school agreements. These were introduced in September 1999 (DfEE 1998) but have no legal status and must not be used as a condition of the child's admission to school (Mansfield 1999). They are seen as a mechanism for promoting positive and productive partnerships between home and school. They also offer possibilities of dialogue with pupils, giving more credibility to the notion of a whole-school policy (Parker-Jenkins *et al.* 2001). They should express in clear, accessible language, the responsibilities on the part of the school and the home. An agreement is reciprocal, providing opportunities for both parties to understand and respect each other's perspectives and responsibilities. However, the findings of Ouston and Hood (2000) and Parker-Jenkins *et al.* (2001) are that the initiative does little to promote home–school partnerships.

CASE STUDY 9.2

The following is an example of a home–school agreement.

Home–School Agreement

Golden Rules

- I will try to be helpful and kind to everyone.
- I will try my best at all times.
- I will be polite to everyone.
- I will take care of things I use.
- I will walk and use a quiet voice inside the school.

Child's signature:

The school will aim to:

- Encourage children to do their best at all times;
- Encourage each child to value and respect each other and their surroundings;
- Provide a balanced curriculum;
- Inform parents of their child's progress through the annual report and at parents' evening;
- Build positive, trusting relationships between staff, children and parents;
- Care for each child's safety and happiness;
- Inform parents about school activities;
- Contact parents if there is a problem concerning their child.

The family will try to:

- Make sure my child arrives at school on time and properly equipped;
- Ensure my child attends regularly and inform the school immediately if my child is absent;
- Support my child's learning at home;
- Attend parents' evening whenever possible;
- Make school aware of any concerns or problems that might affect my child's progress.

Head teacher's signature:

Parent's signature:

CHAPTER 10

Ongoing collaboration between home and school

Key issue
- How can parents and schools continue to work together to support learning once children have started school?

Hughes *et al.* (1994) found that, while parents were generally happy with the school they had chosen for their child, many felt that they did not know enough about what went on at school and would like to know more. Once children have begun school, parents expect to be kept informed about their child, have sufficient access to school and be given a wide variety of opportunities to understand their child's progress and the work of the school.

Schools have long known that parents have a crucial role to play in their child's success within the educational process. Evidence shows that parental support makes a major difference to a child's performance. The Headstart programme and other parental participation programmes have made it clear that the long-term effects of children's development and success are a result of parent–child interaction, the active participation of parents in their children's learning and the expectations that they have of their children (Sylva and Moss 1992). One driving force behind parental partnership, therefore, is the recognition of the need to involve parents if children are to make faster progress. The potential of this partnership in children's learning may be increased when educators see the home as a context for learning, for 'the education system can only become learner-centred by fully recognising that the home is the most significant place of learning in peoples' lives' (Alexander 1996: 17). Meighan and Siraj-Blatchford (1997: 43) maintain that parents can become competent teachers of their children given 'support, advice and guidance'. Hannon and James (1990) note that parents who are not given constructive advice often muddle through with the uneasy feeling that they are doing it wrong. However, once their child has started at school many parents may feel that they have given responsibility for the education of their child over to the teachers (Wolfendale 1989) and feel uneasy about approaching the school for advice.

CASE STUDY 10.1

The following conversation between Lorraine and Debbie shortly after their children had started school emphasises that parents want to support their children and want information on how to do this.

From: <Debbie@ezyfriend.net>
To: <Lorraine@talk.com>
Subject: Communication
Date: October

Dear Lorraine,
   We had all that talking during the induction days, which was far too much. I didn't understand a lot of it and now I've forgotten most of it anyway. We weren't able to meet the teacher so we don't know what she expected. People assume you know just because you've had one start at school but it's different each time. It was quite hard at the beginning finding out who was who. It would have been nice to have had a list and some photos of the staff. And we didn't know about photograph day until that morning because Hayley had forgotten to tell me!
   I feel like once I've taken Hayley to the doorway she's Mrs Brown's. I would've liked to have gone and looked but I've not felt that I've had permission to do so. I don't like to intrude.

Love, Debbie

From: <Lorraine@talk.com>
To: <Debbie@ezyfriend.Net>
Subject: Support with Learning
Date: October

Dear Debbie,
   Stacey doesn't tell me much about school. The first week I hadn't got a clue. I had to learn the right words like number and English. I try to prise it out of her but I'm better not asking. It's as if it's her separate life from home. I wait till she tells me. Little bits come out and all the songs. We pool information from her friends' parents but it's upsetting because I'd like to know.
   I'm here to support her all the way along and do the best I can to help her, but I don't know what to do. The reading record is useful; I know exactly what she's doing there but not in maths whatsoever.

Love, Lorraine

(Adapted from Fabian 1998)

Gaining a picture of school life

It is important to continue to keep channels of information open after children have started school. Hughes *et al.* (1994) found that parents have a paucity of knowledge about what goes on at school in a general sense and would like to know more. They note that parents gather information from, and about, the school in a number of ways but frequently rely on their children as the main source of information. This implies that there is diffidence on the part of parents about asking teachers, even if the staff are welcoming. However, teachers may only see the parent as a 'vehicle for the child' (Alexander 1996: 17) and contact with parents may be limited. Vopat (1994: 8) suggests that many parents feel disaffected from school, many are unsure how they can best help their child succeed, and many have no support or encouragement for their own accomplishments as parents. If this is so, then not only is the desire among parents to be involved with their children's education not being utilised but also an opportunity for parent education is being missed (Smith 1980).

> In order for parents to support the school and to recognise their central educational role, they need to gain a detailed picture of school life, understand just how best they can help their child at home and how they can work in close liaison with the teacher. (Dowling 1995: 23)

Information can be shared by:

- displaying photographs and names of key personnel;
- displaying planning for parents to see the key themes in progress;
- sharing routines with parents by displaying the weekly timetable;
- providing notices to remind parents when PE kit is needed;
- providing oral reports to parents on a day-to-day basis as children are settling in (not always possible if childminders collect children from school);
- displaying information about the best time to talk to the teacher;
- asking parents how their child settled on return to home after being at school;
- having a monthly diary where parents record family events such as visitors and outings.

Parents usually want to know how they can be involved in, and support, their child's learning. This might be done by:

- having interactive displays in the entrance which parents can discuss with their child on the way into school, e.g. a rhyming display where parent and child can read poems together;

CASE STUDY 10.2

Parents' knowledge about school emerges slowly. By the end of the first term at school Debbie and Lorraine are just beginning to gain an understanding:

From: <Debbie@ezyfriend.net>
To: <Lorraine@talk.com>
Subject: Knowledge about school
Date: December

Dear Lorraine,
   Do you know what goes on at school now? We get lots of information by letter, an amazing amount of paper, but little access to the teacher. You feel there's a barrier. I guess they're being professional. The secretary is really helpful, very approachable.
   It's taken me two children to find out what goes on at school. Although Hayley tells me what she does, it would've been nice to know about the topics they do, we could help then, or right at the beginning to have had a piece of paper with 'this is what we do on Monday, Tuesday etc.' just a general outline. It would be nice to go in and sit in on part of the day, too. They could have a rota to come in and watch. If people know what's going on they feel more confident and secure and can use that as a stepping-stone to move on.
   I was pleased we had parents' evening early on because sometimes it's a bit difficult to catch the teacher during the week. You never know what time of day is best and there's no privacy with everyone around. On parents' evening I felt she really knew Hayley but I wanted *her* to tell us more, rather than *us* telling her. They need to be skilled at talking to people and how you say it, don't they?

Deb

From: <Lorraine@talk.com>
To: <Debbie@ezyfriend.net>
Subject: Information about learning
Date: December

Dear Debbie,
   I talked to the teacher in little bits over the first few weeks and I looked in Stacey's books.
   They're always there to help you. The building helps, being open plan, when you walk in you can see the teachers. I can nip in and say whatever; they're so open and approachable. It's good for Stacey to know that I talk to her teacher; it makes her feel more at ease, like a friendship so that she doesn't feel it's separate from home. If she sees that I get on with her teacher, it'll give her more confidence.

But it's still like getting blood out of a stone trying to find out what Stacey does at school. I have to read between the lines. I know the theme but don't know the detail of anything. It's private to her. I find that so frustrating but I suppose she wants to keep school separate from home. Although sometimes, when she's really proud of something, she takes us into the classroom to have a look. And the teacher comes out at the end of the day and talks.

I felt the report didn't say anything academically; we got more on a one-to-one. I enjoyed the first parents' evening. It gave us a good idea of how she was settling in. We were amazed at how much she'd done. The teacher was able to talk about her work in detail. I think that if there were major problems they'd haul me in and tell me, although I'd liked to have known earlier how she was doing socially.

I still find letting go difficult. You have to put your trust in the teachers and the system.

Love, Lorraine

(Adapted from Fabian 1998)

- displaying children's work and photographs with captions explaining the learning gained from the activities, experiences and outcomes. By displaying photographs of interactions parents can see the process and by adding the questions that were asked they might see how the intention to engage with learning is fostered;
- providing link books with suggestions of ways that parents can follow up work in school, although teachers need to have a realistic view about family life and the amount of extra activities that can be accommodated;
- having a drop-in clinic to talk about a focus issue, e.g. writing;
- helping parents to recognise that learning takes place in a wide variety of settings beyond the classroom.

Information about progress

If parents are to support their child's learning, there are implications for teachers to consult with and inform parents. All schools are required to inform parents about progress that their child makes in an annual report and give parents the opportunity to discuss the outcomes of baseline assessment during their first term at school. However, concerns of parents are often more immediate and are helped by a framework for sharing children's achievements both formal and informal. This can happen through:

- inviting parents to add to observations;

- providing for privacy to discuss children's progress when talking to the teacher at the beginning or end of the day;
- giving parents information about their child's progress or any problems that arise;
- having a parents' evening soon after children have started school;
- giving direction on ways in which parents can contribute to their child's learning;
- having regular times when parents can look at their child's recorded work.

Meetings and parents' evenings require confidence on the part of parents to be able to call in at school. To meet children's needs, parents themselves need to be confident individuals (Pugh *et al.* 1994). This may come about through past experiences, home, social position and employment status, but equally it may be to do with the way in which the school develops the well-being of parents. Indeed, Griebel and Niesel (1997) suggest that teachers should act as professional guides for the family. Therefore, an important part of these meetings is to reaffirm the contribution of parents to their children's learning at home. More attention might be given to bringing experiences from home into school and perhaps 'using the school as a resource centre for supporting the home as a place of learning' (Alexander 1996: 17).

Far from increasing, information exchange reduces as children progress through school, with the parents' role becoming supportive and less active. This can bring renewed feelings of uncertainty for many parents for, although they have put their trust in the school, most still want guidance on ways in which to support their child's learning at home. However, parents also feel that, as their child gains in independence, they can reduce their involvement with the school. As a result, the nature of the partnership with school changes.

✎ **Activity 10.1**

Consider how you can develop a successful partnership with parents during the first term that children are in school. The following grid might give you some ideas.

Parental involvement

Type of involvement	Activity
Welcoming parents	• Pre-entry meetings • Photo board of staff and governors • Multilingual signs • Inviting parent volunteers to organise a new parents' coffee morning
Communication	• Home visits • Entry profile information • Newsletters • Staff availability • Home–school diary • Open evenings • Reports • Booklets for parents about aspects of the school and its curriculum
Strengthening parents' voices	• Consultation with parents over issues • Parent-governor attendance at events • Annual governors' report given to new parents
Parents as educators	• Booklets about helping children to learn at home before school • Suggest parents stay with child for first ten minutes of school day and hear them read • Curriculum evenings for new parents • Curriculum displays • Home–school diary
Involving parents in school	• Translating information • Using skills to support work in school • Consultation about needs
Special needs and circumstances	• Follow up concerns raised at entry • Sharing individual education plans • System for informing parents of accidents

CASE STUDY 10.3

Cambridgeshire found that successful partnerships (at secondary level) had five main characteristics:

- open and welcoming;
- communicates clearly and frequently with parents;
- encourages parents as educators and learners;
- gives strength to parental voices in the development of the school;
- responds flexibly to parents' needs and circumstances.

The Cambridgeshire report (Bennet and Downes 1998:13) explores these broad headings in more detail. The following is a summary of the main issues.

Schools that are open and welcome
- pay attention to the physical environment and the reception arrangements for parents;
- check all letters home for clarity of content and friendliness of tone;
- expect all staff to respect and value parents;
- are clear about what can and cannot be expected of parents;
- respond promptly and effectively to parental concerns;
- value *all* parents, irrespective of lifestyle and background.

Schools that are successful in communicating with parents
- are sensitive to parents' needs and do not always work from assumptions;
- are systematic rather than haphazard in their communications;
- create non-threatening opportunities for dialogue;
- recognise that this is an area of work requiring staff development and an input of staff time and resources.

Schools that successfully encourage parents to see themselves both as educators and learners
- are themselves learning organisations committed to professional and personal development;
- provide parents with practical advice on how they can support children with homework;
- are systematic and thorough in exchanging information with parents about the curriculum and about their child's progress;
- act on the belief that all parents are interested in their child's education, regardless of their perceived history or image.

Schools that are responsive to the needs of all parents
- listen as much as they speak;
- have a constructive attitude to complaints and criticism;
- are willing to be vulnerable and to take a few risks;

- require a strong base of shared values, supported by clear aims and policies.

Schools that strengthen the parental voice
- act early to achieve parental involvement;
- show parents how their opinions make a difference;
- create structures which enable less confident parents to participate and contribute;
- build trust through sharing information, successes and problems;
- have an agenda for future action.

PART 4

Settling in to School

CHAPTER 11

Making sense of school

Key issues
- What rites of passage take place at the start of school?
- How do children gain an understanding of the school's culture?

Children come to school with attitudes, expectations and values that are characteristic of their own family structures (Curtis 1986: 155). They then begin a
process of acculturation where they gain an understanding of the school
culture and society through learning the rules, routines and language of the
classroom. Those children with older siblings may have acquired some understanding of the expected school values, mores and systems vicariously. Within
role-play they may have developed 'script knowledge' (Gura 1996: 37) while
they explored 'make-believe' school with others who have had experience of
real school. They may have accompanied an older sibling each day to and from
school. However, for many, and usually for the first child in the family, school
will be a completely new experience. For some children the values and
customs of the classroom may be different from those encountered at home, in
a preschool setting or from any role-play situation. This mismatch may
produce conflict and uncertainty within the child.

Gregory and Biarnes (1994) and Harkness and Super (1994) suggest that
parents' ideas shape their children's behaviour and development. They
propose that it is adults' cultural attitudes that play a central role in the
construction of children's environments for learning to be competent members
of their cultures. This comprises three components:

1. the physical and social settings in which the child lives;
2. culturally regulated customs of childcare and child rearing; and
3. the psychology of the caretakers. (Harkness and Super 1994: 61)

It is through these systems that the child 'abstracts the social, affective, and cognitive rules of the culture' (Harkness and Super 1994: 61). In this way the attitudes and confidence levels of parents are passed on to their children and influence the starting point of the school experience. Even children with similar backgrounds and from the same area come to school with different experiences and differing expectations. They arrive with some knowledge, a diversity of skills and abilities, and where some already have expertise. Even for children arriving on the same day, the experience will be perceived in quite different ways. To become part of school they need to develop a sense of belonging.

Rites of passage

The notion of rites of passage during the induction to school stems from the work of Van Gennep (1960) who explored a number of situations in which the individual passes through transitional stages. He states 'the life of an individual in any society is a series of passages from one age to another and from one occupation to another. Wherever there are fine distinctions among age or occupational groups, progression from one group to the next is accompanied by special acts' (Van Gennep 1960: 3). He suggests that situations are cushioned by rituals and ceremonies, the function of which is to 'enable the individual to pass from one defined position to another which is equally well defined' (Van Gennep 1960: 3). These attendant rites of passage help to incorporate the individual into the group, changing the individual from one status to another. Van Gennep proposes that a complete scheme of rites of passage would theoretically include rites of separation, rites of transition and rites of incorporation.

Rites of passage for children leading up to the start of school are often marked by procedures such as buying and trying on items of school uniform. The night before the first day at school the uniform is sometimes specially prepared. Children wearing their school uniform for the first time marks the rite of the first day of school. There are physical rites during visits to school, such as entering the school building and being shown the environment for the first time, usually during the pre-visits. For some children there is an 'entrance ceremony' when their parents take their photograph at the school gate or as they enter school on the first official day of school. There are social rites such as the first meeting with the teacher, children being introduced to classmates and the 'naming ceremony' of the register. There is the first separation from their parent(s) and meeting them again at the end of the first day.

The induction phase of starting school, comprising any pre-entry activities and the first few weeks of settling in, is a stage in itself. It is a stage that needs to be gone through before balance and routine are once again restored. It is where children and parents 'go from something familiar, habitual and stable through a process of reorganisation until a new stability is reached' (Kell 1992: A8).

At the start of school, children undergo a change in their status and identity with the associated reorganisation of roles and family relationships. There are different expectations associated with their new position in society. Bronfenbrenner states:

> Roles have a magiclike power to alter how a person is treated, how she acts, what she does, and thereby even what she thinks and feels. The principle applies not only to the developing person but to others in her world. (Bronfenbrenner 1979: 6)

There can be confusion about the changing nature of their status. When children are attending pre-entry sessions they are 'being a visitor' and have status because of the special nature of visitors (although many children may think that they have already started school). Once they attend school as a pupil they change status and become a school child, often gaining an identity through wearing their school uniform. This is often accompanied by an increase in confidence. However, they lose their special status when the next set of children start their pre-entry visits. If children are joining an established class they might be unaware that they are joining a group of children who have been at school for some time. The language of size can also cause confusion. Before starting school they are told they are 'big' but when they begin school they are 'one of the little ones'.

Turner outlines the way in which the behaviour of novices is as though they are being reduced or ground down to a level status in order 'to be fashioned anew and endowed with additional powers to enable them to cope with their new station in life' (Turner 1969: 95). He suggests that there is a transient humility where pride is tempered during the transition but also where beginners become a community of equals together and among themselves develop 'an intense comradeship and egalitarianism' (Turner 1969: 96). He notes that in many kinds of initiation the beginners of both sexes are dressed alike and referred to with the same words. For example, those schools that have a school uniform now have similar styles both for girls and boys and the new entrants in many schools may be referred to as 'the new children'. Indeed, some children may find it strange that everyone wears similar clothes and may question why everyone dresses the same. This levelling is partly a destruction of the previous status and partly a preparation in order to cope with their new responsibilities, almost like a blank slate on which to inscribe knowledge of the forthcoming status and to learn a role identity: in this case, the role of pupil in which they 'begin to recognise that their conduct creates expectations, and that they must introduce new social and cognitive competencies into their behavioural repertoire' (Bernard Van Leer Foundation 1993: 13).

CASE STUDY 11.1

The following draws together some observations from Reception class teachers in two schools during the settling-in period at the beginning of term.

Teachers felt that 'it took a good three weeks to get them under control. They couldn't sit on chairs. Establishing working patterns was the hardest.' One teacher said that the first three weeks were 'like a honeymoon period. They're overawed and do exactly as you say, to the letter. But then they start to test you and try the limits.' Another said, 'after three weeks they didn't necessarily behave better, they were just more aware of what was expected'. By half-term the children had become 'more confident and independent'.

Helping children to feel confident, secure and happy were seen as priorities in the first weeks as well as helping them to understand 'what the acceptable modes of behaviour are', usually by repetition and indicating those who are conforming to the model as well as explaining 'this is how we do things in school'. Children were encouraged to become 'responsible for themselves' although staff also felt that it was important that children knew that they could ask if they were unsure.

(Fabian 1998)

Culture

Culture can be defined as 'socially transmitted adjustable behaviour' (De Waal in Bird 2001). Kurtz-Costes *et al.* (1997: 163) note that culture is used 'to represent the values, traditions, behaviors, and beliefs characteristic of a group of people'. Schein (1992 in Neville 1995: 30) suggests it goes beyond *representing* to *teaching* new members the ways of the group:

> A pattern of shared basic assumptions that the group learned as it solved its problems of external adaptation and internal integration, that has worked well enough to be considered valid and, therefore, to be taught to new members as the correct way to perceive, think, and feel in relation to those problems.

The culture in school is not always obvious to children but can be a powerful force in creating expectation and shaping behaviour. Bruner (1996a) proposes that, through participation, children acquire and understand the culture of the organisation. They learn the classroom routines and culture through living it, observing others, copying, asking their friends, listening to or asking the teacher. In this way the culture is absorbed without conscious thought through 'osmosis' (Claxton 1998). By taking part in the life of the school, children construct their own realities and meanings and adapt them to the system, thereby acquiring the school's ways of perceiving, thinking, feeling and carry- ing out discourse. In those classes with established children the teacher often asks older children to look after younger ones and they become role models to teach the culture and appropriate behaviour. The new children become ethnog- raphers, looking at customs, similarities and differences between behaviours. They watch and listen, searching for clues, noting what they see and hear, and then trying to reproduce the observed behaviour and language. However, becoming part of the culture is more than just copying. It is about understand- ing the expressions, body language and culture of people. This 'handover principle' is when the child moves from spectator to participant and begins to take responsibility for their actions (Tharp and Gallimore 1998: 101).

Acculturation suggests that new children are precluded from creating their own culture. The group culture cannot be seen 'simply as a reified or separate entity' (Neville 1995: 32) as individuals bring their own culture (which is often rooted in more than one culture) to the group culture. Some children may put aside the culture of the preschool setting, while bringing some of it with them. Theories developed in one cultural setting also hold elsewhere and if customs are more, rather than less, similar across the two societies, acculturation should occur more easily (Kurtz-Costes *et al.* 1997). When children are active and shar- ing they have an opportunity to participate in creating the classroom culture (Bruner 1996b), but when they are sitting, taking in knowledge, this is not the case.

> [S]chool is a place not just for subject matter teaching but also a place for re-inventing, refurbishing and refreshing culture in each generation . . . During the month of September, i.e. the opening of school, we create a special form of alienation for children . . . School for children is a tremen- dous responsibility to recreate at their level the culture in which they are going to live and they have to recreate it at every level. (Bruner 1996b: 13–14)

Through being actively engaged with their environment not only do chil- dren acquire knowledge of the world but these same interactions contribute to a child's sense of self (Neisser 1993).

> For many children, positive experiences with a culture enhance self- esteem, which in turn better enable the child to step forth assertively in new situations, leading to greater acculturation, and so the cycle contin- ues. (Kurtz-Costes *et al.* 1997: 177)

Perception systems allow for acquisition of knowledge about what things are, with respect to culturally specified meaning. Neisser proposes a second perception system that allows the person to acquire knowledge about categories to which things belong. For example, these may be the rules of behaviour for different aspects of school life such as playtime, lunch-time, assembly and the classroom. Thus people's actions are guided by perception, but also that interaction through engagment and over time informs their perception.

One way in which teachers may help children make sense of the school culture is through 'as if' behaviour where teachers engage children in the 'rules, rituals and opportunities of the classroom by interacting with them as if the children were already aware of the complexity of those rules and rituals' (Edwards and Knight 1994: 14). However, children's different rates of development, of understanding and of language acquisition may mean that there are different interpretations of the same messages. Edwards and Knight (1994) compare this 'as if' behaviour to that of parents 'inducting' very young babies into the family. This behaviour decreases as the child becomes able to act and communicate for him or herself. Teachers can thus be seen as mediators who facilitate the child's entry into a new world. Indeed, Willes (1983) argues that adult approval is one of the key factors in successful initiation into becoming a pupil.

Rules and routines

The cultural system of a classroom affects those who operate within it but routines serve adult purposes for maintaining the social order of the class and are not experienced by children as any immediate concern of theirs (Willes 1983: 70). However, children come to accept and take them for granted within a short time of starting school and soon learn the difference between those behaviours that are acceptable at home and those expected within the classroom setting (Curtis 1986). Indeed, Sherman (1996: 11) found that children were so accepting of the routine they followed that they would not consider an alternative for 'the routine was school'.

There are both implicit and explicit rules to learn. Children must make sense of the new routines and procedures that require them to behave in new ways. For example, they need to understand the lunch-time cafeteria system where they have to make choices quickly. They might not be able to see the choices on offer and just choose the nearest because that is all they can see. Some children may be unnerved and not know what to do if their routine is different; for example, the child who brings lunch money instead of sandwiches but goes without lunch because he or she does not know the system.

Children, on the whole, attempt to please but do not always know the rules. They are often ignorant of them and then get told off and do not know why. Sherman (1996) proposes that children construct their own, often distorted, interpretation of their teacher's words about behaviour. For example, children might have a misconception about the existence of a 'naughty chair' because a child who misbehaved happened to sit on a particular chair.

Children come to school with their own routines. Furthermore they are used to following their own agenda at preschool but sometimes have a more structured agenda at school. At preschool they are able to work at their own pace and to give up or continue as they need. At school, the routines themselves often interrupt the learning and they are not always able to follow a project through (Cousins 1999; Cleave and Brown 1991). Giving children time to become deeply involved in their own interests has important implications for the settling-in process as it helps in getting to know how children learn and what interests them.

✎ Activity 11.1

How do you introduce the rules in your classroom? Are rules about movement in the classroom, talking and social behaviour, work-related issues, safety and use of equipment, introduced in different ways? How are children helped to bring their own culture to the classroom?

CHAPTER 12

Friendships and social well-being

Key issues
- Why are friends important at the start of school?
- How can children be helped at playtime?
- How can children be helped with learning the language of school?

Starting school means having to get acquainted with new adults and children; getting to know new social rules and values (Thyssen 1997). On entering the wider social world of school there is the possibility of making new friends, but it also means entering the world of social comparison, learning the language of school, being able to read social situations and have a social understanding, in order to become a social member. Children's early social experiences with adults and peers are important to an individual's cognitive development, as a child is less likely to learn well and profit from school without the support of friends. Vygotsky's (1978) work demonstrates that children's learning is a social activity which develops through interaction with adults and other children. Development is framed within a context that is socially created at both local and broad societal levels and is affected by the developing nature of the individual (Tudge *et al.* 1997: 74). Furthermore, if children are socially skilled they are more likely to have a succession of positive experiences with other children (Goleman 1996: 223). Teachers have a role in helping children acquire social flexibility, make choices and integrate different experiences to gain a coherent understanding of school.

The way children feel about themselves in relation to their peers and the way they are supported in their settings by adults set the emotional foundations for them to gain confidence for learning throughout their lives. Children are often more confident if they start school with a friend or know someone else in the same class. It also seems likely that new friendships, developed in the context of play and games, can reduce uncertainty at the start of school (Blatchford 1999).

Language

Cleave *et al.* (1982: 114) highlight children's bewilderment at the amount of unfamiliar words and phrases during the first days of school. Making sense of the conventions of social interactions at school is a major task for children (Gura 1996). For example, newcomers have to learn when they may talk to one another and when this is not allowed (Willes 1983: 68). Learning the systems for answering in a group situation by putting a hand in the air and waiting to be asked, what Willes terms 'bidding', has to be learnt.

Much of meaning-making involves language and while it is likely that children will eventually acquire the host language as well as learn what is valued in the new situation, understanding the language of instruction and communication at school quickly is necessary if children are to learn. On entry to school, children are usually operating effectively in their own home and one of the difficulties that practitioners have to manage is the need to 'maintain children's sense of personal effectiveness while they are learning to operate in a context in which the social rules and amount of adult attention will be very different' (Edwards and Knight 1994: 14). If children can 'read' the teacher then they can begin to anticipate the situation. However, to add to the difficulty, there might be unfamiliar words or words used in a different way at school. The 'language of school' may therefore cause difficulties, resulting in children not being able to understand the meaning of a word or sentence used in instructions and information (Curtis 1986: 155). For example, the word 'hall' usually refers to a much larger space at school than at home, and serves a different function. This suggests that teachers' awareness of their own cultural interpretations and ways of speech may help them respond to the differences in children's understanding. The problem becomes more acute with children for whom English is an additional language. They may become socially isolated and unable to develop proficiency in the new language because they cannot socialise (Tabors 1997).

Curtis (1986: 154) outlines that, at home, children learn from an early age to interpret not only verbal communications but also non-verbal gestures and mannerisms which are characteristic of their own environment and culture. According to Trevarthen (1996), children form idiosyncratic communications, learning through copying the mother's voice, facial expression and hands. Non-verbal cues at school, however, may be vastly different and easily misinterpreted.

Friendships

At the start of school some children will want to keep in touch with former friends from preschool or elsewhere who have gone to a different school or who are still at preschool. However, starting school requires children to learn new patterns of behaviour and form additional friends. Indeed, some children find the most important people in school are the other children and it is they who make school worthwhile (Langsted 1994).

Children may have become familiar with the building and some of the systems during the induction to school but developing friendships is a more gradual process. Pollard (1996: 307) asserts that building relationships with other children is a major challenge when children begin to make their way outside the home. Furthermore, Putallaz and Gottman (1981: 116) state that 'a fair number of preschool and elementary school children fail to acquire any friends or only have a few friends at best'. Winterhoff (1997) identifies three sub-systems, within the wider socio-cultural system of development, that constrain friendships. These are '(1) the pool of possible companions, (2) children's social activity settings, and (3) the control network made up of the people who actually exert influence over children's immediate activity' (Winterhoff 1997: 224). He states that it is the organisation and structuring of the social setting that helps to promote friendships. For example, because the selection of children's friends is limited to the class to which they are assigned, their friendships are controlled during lesson time. This is significant not only because children's friendships motivate learning but also for collaborative learning because 'friends show a higher level of cooperation with one another than do acquaintances or children who do not know one another' (Rutter and Rutter 1992: 147). The physical layout of the setting also influences the 'developmental fluidity' of friendships. It either supports or constrains friendships depending upon whether or not children have visual contact with one another (Winterhoff 1997; Corsaro 1981). If the curriculum on offer restricts movement, this may also affect the development of friendships.

Children have different expectations of themselves in different situations and define themselves in relation to the people with whom they are involved (Gura 1996). For example, younger children grow up and form their identities in the wake of their older siblings. Pollard states that their social development should, therefore, 'be seen as being symbiotic rather than just sequential, for each provides a vital element of the social context for the other' (Pollard 1996: 269). Gura (1996) suggests that there is a constantly shifting nature in children's relationships where opposing categories are common such as big and small, younger and older, and where 'sometimes they are in a subordinate role, at other times they are superior or see themselves as equals' (Gura 1996: 36).

Teacher's role

The first teacher has a role to play in scaffolding social relationships for children, teaching social skills and helping children gain social understanding.

Social understanding is linked to a child's experiences of acceptance and rejection but there are complex social skills involved in making and maintaining friends. These include 'the ability to gain entry to group activities, to be approving and supportive of one's peers, to manage conflicts appropriately, and to exercise sensitivity and tact' (Dowling 2000: 23). Differences in social skills lead to differences in participation and opportunities to be actively involved. Children's individual actions early in the school year can affect their social standing later in the year, so it is important for them to get it right at the beginning. Children who make friends easily show generous behaviour whereby they involve others in their play, praise them, and show affection and care. Socially experienced children also learn that, in order to maintain a friendship, they need to recognise when others are upset and do something about it by reconciling arguments or negotiating rules. Chapter 13 explores some ways to help children with these skills.

The process of moving into a new environment and facing a large group of, often unknown, children and adults is a challenge, even for the most sociable children. Cleave *et al.* (1982: 74) identified the amount of differing group sizes that one child in their study experienced during a day:

assembly (whole school)	360
classroom activities	31
playtime (infants only)	170
special pre-reading group	9
television with another class	60
dinner (first sitting)	110

Considerable social understanding is involved in 'reading' the group culture to gain acceptance, in adapting to large group situations where children are expected to learn alongside others, and in gaining membership of smaller groups where they are expected to cooperate and work collaboratively.

In an attempt to help children develop friendships, teachers often assign children to work together in paired activities or employ 'buddy' systems. This strategy works for some children and contributes to the formation of friendships. For others, although they ostensibly develop friends, in reality this is not the case. Further help is needed if children are to find kindred spirits and meet others who are compatible and where, given time, this will lead to friendships. Some strategies that can be employed include:

- using children's names whenever possible so children know the names of others in the class;
- introducing children to one another in circle time and discussing their likes and dislikes;

- helping children to cooperate by suggesting the words to use;
- extending social understanding through role-play.

Other adults in school, such as lunch-time supervisors and classroom assistants, also have a role to play in supporting positive relationships and helping new children to make friends. They need information about:

- handling confrontations and ways to help children overcome them;
- ways to initiate playground games;
- helping children who are shy;
- introducing a 'friends bench' for those children who are on their own in the playground.

✎ Activity 12.1

Devise two ways in which a child who seems lonely may be socially included. Consider the inclusion of 'different' children, for example travellers, ethnic minorities, and children with English as an additional language, as well as girls and boys. Which worked best and why?

Playtime

One of the important features of the physical environment is the playground, which impacts on the social development of children. Noise and volume of 'traffic', sometimes moving at high speed, may make the playground a frightening and stressful place (Ghaye and Pascal 1988: 16). It can be difficult for a child to go into 'a bare playground after he had had access to play equipment all morning' (Brown and Cleave 1994: 17), particularly if the child has interrupted playing to 'go out to play' (Stevenson 1988). New children have to make sense of the type of play at playtime and learn the culture of the playground.

> The new child in the playground is typically a bystander rather than a participant and his activity level is low. (Cleave *et al*. 1982: 138)

Cleave and Brown (1991) found mixed solutions to the problem of playtime from abolishing it altogether, to new entrants who were expected to join the mêlée on their pre-entry visits. Flexible playtime may ease the problem, although it may not be easy to implement in mixed-age classes or it may cause disruption to timetabled outdoor games. Cleave and Brown (1991: 37) found that children enjoyed playtime and that it is an important time in which to negotiate, form and maintain friendships. However:

[B]eneath the benign appearances of children's friendships lies a conceit. The path of friendship is wrought with 'betrayals', 'sudden fickleness', and failed 'wooings'. (Deegan 1996: 6)

As a result of falling out and refused friendships, children are obliged to renegotiate friendships. The playground is the place where this social process can take place, but children often need support in this.

> **✎ Activity 12.2**
> What helps the social processes? How can teachers help children to develop friendships? Observe what happens to children who have been asked to be mentors or who have been asked to look out for children on the playground. How effectively do they play their role and how much does this depend on the way that it has been introduced to them?

CHAPTER 13

Self-esteem and emotional well-being

> **Key issues**
> - What are the common causes of anxiety at the start of school?
> - How can children be empowered and supported through the start of school?
> - What are the indicators of having settled?

No matter when or at what age children begin school, parents and teachers want children to be happy and to have a start that will help them to settle quickly. The way children feel about themselves and the way they are supported by adults sets the foundations for them to gain confidence, feel emotionally secure, ready to meet new challenges, and learn throughout their lives. School provides a context for children to receive feedback from others on their actions. Success at school is more likely when children are 'self-assured and interested; knowing what kind of behavior is expected and how to rein in the impulse to misbehave; being able to wait, to follow directions, and to turn to teachers for help; and expressing needs while getting along with other children' (Goleman 1996: 193). Nevertheless, some children are at risk of not transferring well and may develop problems caused by the stress of not settling in to school. Even a happy, secure and socially skilled child can be overwhelmed when starting school.

Many factors play a critical part in determining the progress that children make in their first year at school. Social factors such as the loss of friends, adults and the familiar routine of the home or preschool can cause stress. Curtis (1986) and Dowling (1988) identified the main causes of distress at the start of school to be the physical environment and the way it affects the child's movements, daily routines and classroom organisation. Furthermore, the nature of the learning experience and the ratio of adults to children can contribute to distress. In this new environment there are often times of uncertainty about what to do, where to go and how to get there.

Cleave *et al.* (1982: 157) identified particular times of the day such as play-time, lunch-time and assembly as causing anxiety. Many children find assembly difficult. Brown and Cleave (1994) and Dowling (1995) question whether it makes sense 'that one of the first experiences of school for many nursery children is attending a special assembly'. There is certainly conflict between a gentle start to the day followed by a formal assembly, especially if the hall is situated some distance from the classroom. Another area of concern is lunch-time.

> Dinner at school represents more than a major discontinuity in the experience of young children: for most of them it is a totally new experience. (Cleave *et al.* 1982: 140)

Children may have to eat unfamiliar food in unfamiliar surroundings. Because they are unable to identify the foods, some children just eat one food that they recognise, day after day. In some instances, children cannot see what food is available as the counter is too high. The use of different cutlery may prove difficult, and there are also cultural differences in what and how people eat. During the long playtime at lunch-time, Cleave *et al.* (1982: 138) found that new children appeared lethargic and listless. Other areas that have an unsettling effect include:

- not having friends (Fabian 1998);
- commuting by bus. Travel extends the day, particularly for children from rural areas;
- dark mornings and nights during the winter months;
- sitting still. Wiltsher (2000) identified the ability to be still as the most advanced stage of movement, yet sometimes when children start formal schooling they are expected to sit still for long periods;
- a break in attendance due to illness or a holiday (Dalli 1999);
- joining an established class (Hughes *et al.* 1979).

Symptoms

Barrett's (1986) study of children starting school highlights some of the lack of control that children feel when they start school. This can result in physical, psychological and behavioural symptoms such as mood swings, muscle tension, changes in sleeping patterns, low self-esteem or poor concentration. Kienig (1998) found signs of anxiety manifested in the following behaviour disorders in children in Poland at the beginning of school:

- disturbances in basic physiological needs (eating disorders, sleep disorders, bed-wetting);

- emotional reactions (anger and aggression, or withdrawal and depression);
- disturbances in social relationships (inattention, clinging behaviour);
- disturbances in self-care skills (refusal to engage in self-care);
- disturbances in play activities (destructive behaviour regarding toys, aggressive play).

CASE STUDY 13.1

The following case study of Amy settling into school comes from a discussion with Amy's mother that took place six months after Amy had started school.

Amy started school in September. She was an only child from a stable home. She had several friends and achieved well academically. She was tall for her age and looked older than the other children. She appeared confident and the teacher felt that she had settled in to school well, mixing with the others, succeeding with her work and progressing well. Her mother also felt that Amy had settled as she 'was used to being away from home. She can't wait to go to school in the mornings. When I pick her up from school at home time I have to drag her away.' However, after a few weeks Amy was anxious and stressed. These anxieties were not seen at school, but at night she was bed-wetting and having nightmares. This caused not only more stress for Amy but for her parents, too. When Amy and her mum talked it through, it was found that an increase in workload meant that there was no time left for Amy to choose what she wanted to do after she had finished her directed work. A meeting with the teacher soon resolved the problem.

What helps the settling-in process?

Parents can act as a transitional link between home and school, helping their child by talking about it and integrating the two worlds. One of the most important factors is a welcoming, accepting and supportive attitude by the teacher and support staff. The way in which children are introduced to their new environment affects their ability to settle in well. While the differences between preschool and school can be considerable, the nature of the support that a child receives in dealing with discontinuities may be more important than maintaining continuity (Ghaye and Pascal 1988).

Young children learn to make sense of their world through active interaction with it, through observation, exploration, experimentation and mimicry. During the early stages of starting school, children develop an awareness of their environment and know their surroundings through being encouraged to recognise objects such as books that they might know or 'landmarks' round the school. Many schools have a range of equipment that reflects different cultures from around the world. Although materials from other cultures are of value in settling in, they are not the most significant aspect.

> A distressed child cannot be helped by the variety of toys around them, however enticing and attractive they may be. These children require sensitive care and careful guidance . . . (Day 1995: 12)

Exploring the environment with a friend can be beneficial. Becoming familiar with the culture, the environment and the people in it help children to feel 'at home' and comfortable at school. When children know that they are accepted and understood, they are likely to feel part of the organisation.

Transitional objects

Children are 'border-crossers' who make a daily transition between home and school (Campbell Clark 2000). The culture at home and school frequently contrast, making it difficult for some children to settle easily. These boundaries between home and school are marked and strengthened by 'border work' – routine rituals that take place at the beginning and end of the day such as registration, saying goodbye or greeting.

Many children need the reassurance of a teddy or object such as a blanket to sleep. It gives them security and helps them feel safe. The same applies in bringing a special toy to school. It comforts and links the child with other people, especially parents and family, when they are apart (Bruce 1996). Winnicott (1974) calls these 'transitional objects'. Campbell Clark (2000) has identified 'permeations' which cross between domains. These are two-way elements and attitudes that permeate between home and school, such as singing songs at home that are learned at school, carrying family pictures to school and transferring insights from one situation to another. Educators of young children need to recognise the importance of these permeations for the emotional stability that they bring for the child, and treat them sensitively. Not all children will have or need transitional objects but teachers need to consider how they will deal with those that are brought to school. Rather than putting them away out of sight, they might be better in the open where they can be seen and the child allowed to handle them as needed.

Resilience

Laevers *et al.* (1997: 15) describe children with high levels of well-being as feeling 'like fish in water' in their educational environments and having the ability to maximise their learning potential. Csikszentmihalyi (1990) identifies this time when everything comes together well in terms of 'flow', describing it as representing 'the ultimate in harnessing the emotions in the service of performance and learning. In flow the emotions are not just contained and channelled, but positive, energized, and aligned with the task at hand' (Csikszentmihalyi in Goleman 1996: 90).

To achieve this all-round functioning level, each individual's basic needs must be satisfied. Laevers *et al.* (1997) propose that these include physical needs; the need for affection, warmth and tenderness; the need for safety, clarity and continuity; the need for recognition; the need to experience oneself as competent; and the need for life to have meaning. Children need to feel at one with their environment and the people in it, but problem-free lives would make children less able to cope with the challenges that they will inevitably face (Long 2001). Giving children the skills to cope with pressures will enable them to develop the necessary understanding and skills to manage stress effectively. Resilient and emotionally literate children have some sense of mastery over their lives.

Many children enjoy change and adapt easily to transitions, but results of research by Fthenakis and Textor (1998) indicate that there is a need to teach children to cope with transitions by being taught competencies of resilience. Resilience has been defined as 'normal development under difficult conditions' (Fonagy *et al.* 1994: 231–57). This capacity of children to cope successfully with stress and have the resilience to bounce back and to keep going when things are difficult starts with the development of key personal qualities. Krovetz (1999: 7) states that resilient children usually have the following four attributes in common:

- social competence;
- problem-solving skills;
- autonomy;
- a sense of purpose and future.

Goleman (1998: 229) suggests that helping people to develop skills of rapport, empathy, persuasion, cooperation and consensus building fosters a good start and the ability to succeed. This emotional literacy, defined by Sharp (2001: 45) as 'the ability to recognise, understand, handle, and appropriately express emotions', encompasses self-awareness, the motivation to learn, the ability to form relationships, communication skills and resourcefulness to meet new challenges (Goleman 1996). The skills that equip children for dealing with new situations are largely included in the area of personal, social and emotional development of the Foundation Stage (QCA 2000). Ofsted suggests the following expectations for five-year-olds' personal, social and emotional development:

- dispositions and attitudes;
- self-confidence and self-esteem;
- making relationships;
- behaviour and self-control;
- self-care;
- sense of community. (Ofsted 2000: 9)

Teaching emotional literacy

Sharp (2001) has identified aspects of emotional literacy that are both lived and able to be taught in schools:

- conscious awareness;
- understanding thoughts, feelings and actions;
- managing feelings;
- promoting self-esteem;
- managing conflict;
- understanding groups;
- communication skills.

He cites examples where children have been helped with these through games, simulations, puppets, pictures, photographs, stories and cartoons. For example, story can be employed to give actions and objects a context and meaning for children. This helps children with assessing situations quickly and gaining strategies for solving problems.

The peer group can contribute to sharing and making meaning. Circle time, when pupils sit in a circle, assume equal responsibility and operate within an agreed framework of guidelines, can contribute to understanding as children listen to others' explanations and ideas. They can also express their own thoughts in a safe environment. These opportunities for sharing information, discussing feelings and things that happen at school, and how they would like things to be, help to create the culture.

Indicators of settling

The emotional transition starts some time before children start school and lasts longer than many teachers and parents expect. Most children take between three and six weeks to settle in to school, with some settling from the first day and several taking much longer. Some parents are surprised if major changes occur in their child's behaviour at home during the first few weeks of school. Others are surprised at how quickly their children settle, but are unprepared for their children becoming unsettled later if this happens (Fabian 1998).

In interviews with Dalli (1999: 61), mothers indicated that their child had settled by comments such as:

- She doesn't cry when I leave.
- She's able to be with adults other than myself.
- She talks about her teacher.
- She doesn't mind when I leave.
- He ran to the door.
- She's not in a great hurry to get away.

CASE STUDY 13.2

Six Reception class teachers were interviewed about their understanding of when children had settled. They felt the children were beginning to settle when 'they were happy to leave mum and start to make friends and go to each other's houses after school'. A further indicator was that they were able to speak to the teacher and were aware of the routines.

Children were happier and more confident if they took something from the home environment with them, and once they had formed friendships. If a child was with preschool friends, this was significant in helping them to settle.

Staff helped children to develop friendships by using their names, introducing them to one another, consciously grouping them in particular ways, pairing at playtime or for responsibilities. However, one teacher thought that encouraging close friendships too early 'can exclude other children and set up problems'.

Learning to be part of a group was seen as an important part of settling in. Constant repetition helped 'to lay the ground rules' and establish routines, such as putting up their hand if they wanted to speak. Being confident with moving to and from the hall for assembly, lunch, PE and music, and between activities, was also an indicator. Playtime, lunch-time and assembly were explained beforehand and often discussed afterwards. Split playtimes helped with the amount of children on the playground but upset those whose older siblings were not on that 'shift'.

Staff who taught a mixed Reception and Year 1 class thought that it was useful for the Reception children to have the 'older ones to follow'. One teacher bemoaned the fact that there were 'no role models' for the intake who entered a class made up entirely of new Reception children.

(Adapted from Fabian 1998)

✎ Activity 13.1

What can you do to help children settle in to your class as the term progresses?

PART 5

Continuity during Transitions and Transfers

CHAPTER 14

Transitions and transfers: within-phase, cross-phase and pupil mobility

---

Key issues
- What transitions and transfers do pupils make during their formal schooling?
- What issues do transitions and transfers raise?

Transitions occur throughout childhood. They occur as a young child moves from home to an early years setting and from an early years setting to school. During their school years, children experience a number of transitions moving from one class to another, sometimes with different children, a different teacher and to a different room. Pupils also make the transfer between phases of education, for example from infants to juniors, and from primary to secondary school. Cleave and Brown (1991: 214) suggest that head teachers are unlikely to perceive the induction to school in isolation. However, schools usually have a separate induction policy and may therefore not see this as part of a continuum. This indicates that giving consideration to the various points of transition, not only to the initial induction to school but to those transitions through and out of the school, might also be significant and worthy of scrutiny.

> The frequent transitions of childhood provide strategic points of analysis since during them past, present and future are symbolically represented.
> (James and Prout 1997: 234)

There are a growing number of pupils transferring between schools. They move between the state and private sectors and between countries. Pupil turnover is associated with the armed forces, refugees, travellers, occupational travellers, moving house for employment reasons, family breakdown and temporary accommodation. Further turbulence comes about from exclusions and poor attendance, resulting in interrupted learning. These factors can be grouped into four broad categories which comprise:

- **International migration:** families coming and going for employment reasons, refugees and asylum seekers, families arriving or leaving for settlement reasons (e.g. to join relatives) and students with children.
- **Internal migration:** people moving for employment reasons, housing reasons, life cycle reasons (i.e. a particular point in life where a change of home/environment is wanted) and for reasons to do with perceived quality of schools. Travellers are also a distinct group of migrants.
- **Institutional movement:** movement generated by and within the education system (not involving a move of home), such as exclusions, voluntary transfers, private/state school movement and special/mainstream movement.
- **Individual movement:** movement of children between adults and locations, for example when a family has broken up. There are also children in care. (Dobson 2000)

Pupils in transition do not necessarily leave or join at the end of a year, nor at the end of a term. They are just as likely to leave or join at the end of a week or part-way through a year, and often arrive unannounced (Jordan 2000). As they move from one school to another they gain experience but the more changes of school that a child makes, the more opportunities there are for 'dropping out'. There are also more schools responsible for pupils' success or failure. This mobility results in enormous pressures among school communities.

The transitions and transfers that pupils make during their formal schooling are likely to include:

- a daily transition coming to school in the morning and going home at the end of the day. This might involve being met by a parent or being met by a carer/grandparent and then another transition back home later;
- an occasional transition of back-up childcare before or after school if the usual childminder is unavailable;
- transition from school to out-of-school-hours activities (either in the school building or elsewhere) before going home;
- transition at the end of a year to a new classroom, sometimes with different pupils and often to a new teacher;
- cross-phase transfer between key stages;
- mid-year transition.

Some children might experience two transitions at the same time, for example a change of family and a change of school. Occasional transitions are incurred by those families that are home-educating as they sometimes choose to send their children to school for certain lessons or for some of the school year, although this is rare (Meighan 1997).

For children who change schools, there are three steps in the transfer process that coincide with the stages of preparation, separation and integration at the start of school. These comprise a disengagement phase, an interim stage and a reintegration phase (Ballinger 2000). If the move takes place suddenly, there is only a brief disengagement phase. For those who have prior knowledge of the move, such as the armed forces who know about their posting some months in advance, the disengagement phase is characterised by spending more time and energy preparing to leave the culture than in trying to live in it. However, Ballinger (2000) suggests that, once relocated, it can take up to 12 months before the individual has fully engaged with the new culture. She outlines (Figure 14.1) a cycle comprising involvement, leaving, transition, entering and re-involvement that children go through during each transfer (Ballinger 2001).

Transition within a phase

Some parents and children see the routine transitions as an annual upheaval and a necessity that must be endured. For a few they are a relief and a promise of a new beginning. In small schools where there is often only one teacher in each key stage, there is no annual change and this is seen as an aid to pastoral care, but in most primary schools children change classrooms and teacher every year, causing confusion in some families over the 'route' their child takes through school. The Edison Project suggests that this routine change of teachers brings few benefits and reduces continuity (Elkin 1998). Certainly in business a manager who has developed fruitful working relationships with a group of clients would not be expected to change them for another group after just 12 months.

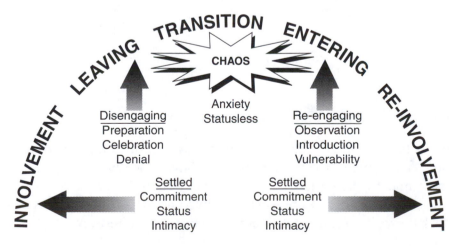

Figure 14.1 The Transition Experience (Ballinger 2001 adapted from Stevens 1998)

CASE STUDY 14.1

Transitions through Key Stage 1 for one child meant five changes in three years, with three of these taking place in his first year at school.

September (Reception)
James joins the Reception class with two job-share teachers.

January (Reception)
He is joined by the January intake.

April (Reception)
The class is split. James stays in the same room with some of the January intake and one of the teachers. Some of the January intake move to another room with the other teacher and the summer intake.

September (Year 1)
James moves to a new room with a different teacher. He goes with some pupils from his class, some from the 'split' class and joins some who have been in the new classroom for a year.

September (Year 2)
James stays with the same teacher in the same room. The previous Year 2 pupils move to another class and Year 1 children and the summer-born Year 2 children join him.

When new children joined the class in January there was disruption to both groups. The new children found it noisy and crowded and the established children felt the new ones were impinging on their territory and they received less time from the teacher. In schools where children stay in one class throughout a key stage, although the teacher has to consider a wider range of developmental needs, he or she is able to get to know the children and parents well and provide continuity.

(Adapted from Fabian 1998)

Transfer between phases: from infant to junior

Children's feelings about changing phases are generally a mixture of nervousness and excitement. Even though they have usually visited their new classroom and teacher briefly, they have not yet developed a working relationship and are unsure of the workload. In some instances, far from calming anxieties, the visit can raise a number of unanswered questions.

CASE STUDY 14.2

Let us look at the conversation between three friends who are about to transfer between the Key Stage 1 and Key Stage 2 phases of their education. Stacey and Stephanie are at a primary school; Hayley is at an infant school and is transferring to a junior school nearby.

Stacey: We're going to the juniors after the holiday. It'll be fun.

Hayley: So am I! Isn't it exciting? I feel a little bit good and a little bit sad.

Stephanie: Yes. We'll have to say goodbye to Mrs Grey. I'll miss all my little friends and the teachers.

Hayley: Me too. It's very big and I might be nervous. People will stare when you're new.

Stacey: And there'll be bullies.

All together: Ugh!

Stacey: Are you going to be in the same class as Emma?

Hayley: Yes! And I've got some friends already up there. And my brother's there.

Stephanie: Me and Stacey'll be in different classes again. We'll only see each other at playtime. We'll make new friends, though. Have you been to see your new school?

Hayley: We've seen a bit. The big girls and boys showed us. We're going to visit again and stay for an hour!

Stacey: We usually have a look around before we move up. Mrs Grey'll take us soon and we'll meet our new teacher.

Hayley: I hope mine's going to be nice and friendly. I hope she doesn't shout. She's got ginger hair and she's tall.

Stacey: Mine's going to be kind.

Stephanie: Samantha thinks ours is going to be bossy and give you lots of homework.

Hayley: We'll have to be really quiet and have to be much more behaved.

Stephanie: And you have hard work and you can't ask for words!

Stacey: You won't be able to choose. The moment you finish one piece of work you have to start another piece!

Hayley: I want to see some of the work to see how hard it is. P'raps if we did hard work now it'd be easier when we get there.

Stacey: Or we could do a topic about Mrs Grey next term.

Hayley: The teachers could come and visit us!

(Fabian 1998)

In the case study above, parents who were interviewed saw the transfer as a big step for themselves but a natural progression to the next 'life-stage' for their children. Parents envisaged few problems in the transition but identified some that might occur:

- using the toilets;
- the lunch-time system;
- the collection of money and other routine domestic arrangements in the first few days;
- missing friends left behind in Key Stage 1 or who have moved to other classes;
- bullying from older children;
- forgetting what they had learned at Key Stage 1 over the long summer holiday;
- coping with an increased and different workload.

Transfer between phases: from primary to secondary

Pupils have already made considerable progress in their primary schools. Many will know how to learn and will be keen to continue doing so at secondary school. They are likely to experience a sense of leaving childish things behind (Rudduck 1996). As they approach secondary education many will be full of excitement at the prospect of specialised accommodation and taking up new subjects such as modern foreign languages. Others may be apprehensive about their ability to cope with new demands, especially if they have had to struggle to maintain their progress at primary school. Many will have to travel some distance to their new school, possibly on public transport. Nearly all will be entirely unused to the kind of organisation and timetabling arrangements that they will encounter in this next phase (Morrison 2000). The turbulence of transfer can create social anxieties and reduce pupils' commitment to learning and steady academic progress (Galton *et al.* 1999a).

The secondary school in partnership with its feeder primary schools needs to consider how it can make the transfer from primary to secondary education as smooth as possible by trying to ensure that children's confidence and sense of well-being are protected. Research by Morrison (2000) found peer support to be effective in this transfer. Pupils from Year 7 sent accounts of their school via email to Year 6 pupils in their former school. These accounts offered a realistic balance of excitement and anxiety in the new setting.

Individual transfer

School transfer might be concurrent with family trauma or be associated with a fresh start. For those children who move some distance from their previous home, there can be an enormous sense of loss. Although the adults might welcome the move to a different house and area, the child might not. They will have to adjust to a new home as well as a new school. The familiar sights, sounds and smells that have been an important and comforting part of their lives are left behind. Even if children stay in the same area, they might lose contact with their friends. There might be new travel arrangements to get to the new school, and a loss of a familiar routine which can result in distress. Feeling connected is important but might be difficult to achieve for isolated learners. A shared history is missing and bonding by sharing experiences has yet to occur.

Children moving to the UK from another country might have special difficulties during the settling-in period. For minority ethnic children, the move represents not only a new environment and unfamiliar people, but also a strange culture and a new language.

McPake and Powney identified four principal areas of dissonance for Japanese pupils when transferring from one educational culture to another:

1. understanding the role of talk and silence in the classroom;
2. the relative importance placed on knowledge and skills for learning;
3. expectations of academic achievement and educational aspirations; and
4. notions of cultural identity. (McPake and Powney 1998: 169)

Stead *et al.* (1999: 5) came to the view that there are issues that apply particularly to refugee pupils, although not exclusively to them:

- the experience of trauma – physical and/or emotional – accompanying departure from the home country and arriving in the UK (this may last for some time and restrict the ability of parents, initially, to engage fully in the education of their children, as they may also be preoccupied with 'survival' issues such as housing/finance/work/training);
- 'not knowing' whether they would be allowed to stay (the process of claiming asylum lasts anything from a few months to several years) and the tension of 'living in two countries simultaneously';
- the possible disruption of education before leaving the home country and on arrival in the UK;
- the 'hidden' aspects of life and values which some families may be

unable, or unwilling, to disclose to others in this country, which can lead to some degree of family introversion;

- the experience of loss of material possessions and status, as well as emotional losses, which may generate a very high degree of commitment to the education of children as a means to securing their future and 'insuring' them against such experiences in the future.

Mobility does not necessarily have a negative effect as pupils also gain experience and benefits because they can:

- become adaptable and flexible;
- become confident with change;
- gain a wide network of friends and value relationships;
- develop a sense of realism and the importance of 'now';
- become adept at closure skills. (Adapted from Pollock and Van Reken 1999)

✎ **Activity 14.1**
Consider ways that you can support individuals who transfer to your class.

CHAPTER 15

Transfer and academic progress

Key issues
- What impact does transfer have on learning?
- What are the factors affecting transfers and transitions?
- How might children be helped to continue and develop their learning capability during transfer and transitions?

It is important to look at and understand more about the impact that transitions have on performance and attitudes in learning as pupils move from one year to another and from one school to another. The impact of high mobility can be an obstacle to raising achievement and causes inconsistencies in school results. Certainly the underachievement of traveller pupils is attributed to lack of curriculum continuity and coherence in their education (Jordan 2000; Ofsted 1999). Many schools devote their energy towards efforts aimed at smoothing the transfer process rather than ensuring that pupils remain committed to learning and progress (Galton *et al.* 1999a). It is estimated that two out of every five pupils fail to make the progress that could be expected during the year immediately following a change of school. The National Children's Bureau (Madge 2001) found that children who find the process especially difficult include those with English as an additional language or with special needs, particularly if they feel they are getting less support than previously. Entitlement to continuity, therefore, needs to be recognised. How can schools ensure continuity of learning for children on the move?

Factors determining successful transitions and transfers

Van Gennep (1960) and Claxton (1998) suggest that having recognised something on one occasion makes it easier to recognise again, as there is a residual effect of the first recognition that facilitates the second. The second time that something occurs it is processed as a memory rather than as a fresh perception and it is identified and categorised faster. This suggests that each move becomes easier. However, regardless of the number of moves, there are some factors that affect each transfer:

- attitude and levels of confidence about the move;
- type of learner;
- continuity of individual relationships and friendship groups;
- preparation by home and school.

Levels of confidence

Chislett (2001) identifies the need to prepare children for transfer by helping them understand the emotional dimension of change. Galton *et al.* (1999a) acknowledge that pupils need help to increase their ability to handle the challenges of transfer and to thrive on it. Levels of confidence are often influenced by home circumstances but the transfer itself might have a negative impact on pupils, leading to loss of confidence in themselves as learners. For example, a dependence on the teachers and the school for learning can lead to a loss of motivation. If the teacher controls learning too much, pupils become dependent on the teacher and lose much of their ability for independent self-motivated learning. Education needs to create a range of social and intellectual skills that enable pupils to be self-reliant, creative, enterprising, flexible and able to cope with ambiguity. These higher order skills include the ability to hypothesise, weigh evidence, categorise, synthesise, evaluate arguments, make judgements, solve problems and reflect critically upon experience (Long 2000).

Type of learner

Experiences gain significance against a background of earlier social and cultural occurrences. Research has shown that people have different approaches to learning according to the way that the learning episode is experienced. The approach adopted by an individual is a combination of the way in which the learning and the learning situation are experienced, based on previous experience. These experiences have a bearing on behaviour as people act on the basis of their experience. Children do not choose their view of life, but develop their values according to their experiences and the values of those around them. Thus learning is seen as how someone experiences, sees or makes sense of the world (Pramling Samuelsson *et al.* 2000).

The amount of information that pupils require on transfer and the way in which they deal with transfer might be to do with learner 'types'. Claxton (1998: 73) cites the work of Wescott who identifies four different groups of learners. There are those who typically require very little information before offering a solution, and who are likely to be correct. These he calls the 'successful intuitives'. There are those who ask for little extra information but who tend to be wrong. These are the 'wild guessers'. The third group require lots of information before being willing to respond, but are generally successful when they do. These are the 'cautious successes'. Finally there are those who make use of all the information they can get, but who still make a lot of mistakes. These are the 'cautious failures'. Children's personalities and the way they view new situations, therefore, might make a difference to the way in which they settle into a new environment.

Continuity of friendships

Children change schools and classes in groups and individually. A high level of social confidence often helps to make the transition an easier one. Friendship groups promote a degree of security and help emotional well-being during times of stress (Rutter and Rutter 1992).

Peer groups have a special significance because many children can expect to be with the same group of children for several years. This provides a sense of continuity in the midst of change (Gura 1996). Cleave and Brown (1991) found that for children to be in the same class for two years enabled friendships to be developed and gave children a feeling of stability. However, it is not always possible to maintain the same groups of children through school, due to circumstances such as the number of children and fluctuating staffing allocations that determine the type of class organisation adopted. If transition causes disruption to some friendship pairs and groups, this is not always a disadvantage as sometimes new relationships form as a result. Nonetheless, Gura (1996) and Langsted (1994) outline the importance for children of other children in school. As an emotional resource 'friendships furnish children with the security to strike out into new territory, meet new people, and tackle new problems' (Hartup 1991: 1). Therefore making, having and keeping friends must be planned for as part of a whole curriculum. However, teacher attitudes and practices about friendship can influence friendship development patterns (Winterhoff 1997: 246).

Preparation for transitions

Galton *et al.* (1999a) have confirmed that progress 'dips' for a sizeable majority of pupils after transfer to secondary school. When pupils are prepared for making transitions they gain self-confidence and are more likely to succeed. However, they also need to sustain an enthusiasm for learning, have confidence in themselves as learners and continue learning throughout the transition. Galton *et al.* (1999b) point out that in the five main categories of transfer activity there is little focus on parts 4 and 5:

1. *Administrative approaches* which highlight exchanges of information, usually at the level of the individual teacher, or organisational

approaches which bring pyramid schools together in a working relationship.

2. *Pupil-centred approaches* which concentrate on preparing pupils for
   the social upheaval of transfer and help them cope with the new school.
3. *Curriculum continuity approaches* which involve exchanges of material and teachers or which may involve pupils in projects that start in
   Year 6 and are completed in Year 7 in the new school.
4. *Pedagogic approaches* which seek to engage pupils by involving them
   in new ways of teaching and learning.
5. *Approaches that give priority to exploring and explaining the purpose
   and structure of learning in the new setting* (including, perhaps, ways
   of assessing and improving learning) and that recognise pupils' needs
   – and capacity – to develop a language for thinking about learning and
   about themselves as learners.

(Galton *et al.* 1999b: 3)

Boyd and Simpson (2000) also found that schools in Scotland are having
difficulty with curricular continuity at transfer. Not only are ways needed,
therefore, to reduce the impact of social and emotional turbulence but also
ways to maintain levels of attainment and help pupils continue learning
during pre-transfer, transfer and post-transfer. The following activities might
be helpful in supporting the transfer.

Pre-transfer

- Present a picture of the coming year which helps pupils look forward with
  excitement to the learning that will take place.
- Provide opportunities to talk through the way pupils view the forthcoming
  transfer and learning in the year ahead.
- Ensure pupils know the name of their teacher before the move and meet him
  or her if possible either face-to-face or on the Internet.
- Help pupils get to know pupils in the next class, possibly through video
  conferencing.
- Provide taster days with an opportunity to do some work and see examples
  of work.
- Receive an induction pack from the next school.
- Ensure pupils are aware of the transfer process.
- Arrange counselling sessions to provide an opportunity to talk through feelings. Sometimes pupils start to feel negative about where they are or create
  conflicts to ease the pain of separating (Ballinger 2001).
- Set up 'Futures' counselling sessions to encourage pupils to talk about
  where they are going and previous moves that they have made. In this way
  pupils can learn from each other's successes and think constructively about
  the future.

- Arrange a weekly group session with other pupils who will be transferring/ entering the same class.
- Support the 'non-movers' in the class. They might prepare an induction pack for new pupils or receive mentor training.
- Read stories about moving.
- Discuss how pupils might tackle unfamiliar situations.
- Talk with pupils who have gone through the process previously.
- Establish email links with the new school to exchange information and start to develop friendships (Morrison 2000).
- Access the next school's web site to gain an understanding of the new school.
- Outline the opportunities available to become more responsible. For example, describe clubs that they can join.
- Conduct study support groups to learn about learning at the next stage.
- Have a joint project with the next school in the term before transfer.
- Help pupils develop reliable work habits (Rudduck 1996).
- Develop induction programmes that involve parents.
- Have a 'leavers' assembly (although this farewell ritual can be upsetting).

During/between transfer
The feeder school and receiving school can work together by:

- continuing pupil–pupil exchange of information through email;
- holding summer schools;
- informing receiving schools of test results and progress, e.g. through transferring records with the child;
- having an induction course for new pupils which outlines the way in which teaching and learning take place and begins to develop a language for thinking about themselves as learners (Rudduck 1996);
- having induction training for teachers.

Post-transfer
- Have a welcome ceremony.
- Encourage new pupils to talk about where they have transferred from.
- Provide information about the daily classroom routine, e.g. any special clothing and equipment required.
- Check for 'gaps' in learning but do not assess for learning immediately.
- Organise visits (face-to-face or by Internet) by the previous teacher to see the children.
- Track to check whether the more able pupils are being challenged sufficiently.
- Develop structures to allow pupils to ask questions about things they do not understand, their concerns about learning and teacher expectation, e.g.

through conversation circles or written questions. Once fears are acknowledged and shared they lose some of their power.

- After the 'holiday' feel wears off, help pupils to find similarities and form links.
- Have a mentoring programme that involves pupils (this could start before transfer).
- Support teachers in developing skills to evaluate the impact of transfer and transition.

Individual transfers

Most of the situations above refer to groups of pupils transferring, but for pupils transferring individually there are often different needs both for pupils and schools:

- provision of uniforms and equipment (Bhopal *et al.* 2000);
- race equality and equal opportunities policies to demonstrate an inclusive ethos in the school and reassure parents;
- culturally relevant learning materials;
- sanctuary areas;
- respecting the language and culture of transitory communities;
- parents and pupils understanding how pupils are allocated to classes (Stead *et al.* 1999);
- understanding the education system and curriculum;
- distance learning to smooth gaps for interrupted learners.

> ✎ **Activity 15.1**
> Tell the class a story about a pupil who is transferring to another school and a situation with which he or she is faced (for example, a social situation on the playground). Give three or four options of how the pupil might behave. In pairs ask the class to choose one or suggest one of their own that they think would help the new pupil and give reasons for their choice.

Support for parents of transitioners

Parents can be supportive and a source of security as they are a known reference point in an unknown environment and give continuity between contexts (DES 1990). They are a 'common factor' person who helps to link the old and new and give a role model of social behaviour (Bronfenbrenner 1979). However, preparation for parents is also important otherwise anxiety is likely to be created, particularly if parents do not know where to take their children or if they have no knowledge of the expected system. Most parents want clear communication and preparation for themselves as well as their children at each transition. If parents have sufficient information, they feel able to ease the transitions for their child.

CASE STUDY 15.1

In a survey of 50 parents whose children were transferring between Key Stage 1 and Key Stage 2, parents felt that they had helped their children with the transfer in a number of ways:

- talking with their children about the move;
- finding out about the new school;
- walking through the grounds;
- finding out which friends would be in the same class;
- maintaining normal routines;
- giving them encouragement;
- listening to their worries;
- giving their child some control by letting them decide when to buy the new uniform;
- emphasising the positive.

(Adapted from Fabian 1998)

CHAPTER 16

Monitoring and evaluating induction and transitions

Key issues
- How can the effectiveness of the induction programme be evaluated?
- Who is involved with monitoring and evaluating the programmes?

Schools want effective induction systems that help children to enter school, settle quickly and continue learning. School is no longer seen as a system that others have to fit but as a merging of school and family into a partnership, where the coordinator is a team leader making connections for the child between the home, preschool and school. To meet this ideal it is worth taking time to consider and evaluate the procedures of induction and any induction policy by gaining the perceptions of children, parents and teachers. The issue for schools is to identify the prime purpose of their induction system and examine its adequacy in terms of:

- how well children settle;
- the impact of the transition on pupils' motivation and learning;
- how well pupils cope with further changes.

This process includes monitoring and evaluating:

- the induction policy for those beginning school and transferring into the school at other points;
- the marketing materials;
- the pre-start transition programme;
- the admissions procedure;
- the management of:
  - transitions of classes/groups/individuals through school;
  - cross-phase transfers;
  - transfer of incoming individuals/groups from other schools;

   – transfer of outgoing individuals/groups to other schools;
- parental involvement with transitions and transfers;
- the role of the induction coordinator.

Who monitors and gathers the evidence will depend on what is being monitored. Some aspects are best done by the head teacher, for example processes concerned with transfer. Performance management processes that involve team leaders can be used to gain the views of teachers. The induction coordinator and Reception class teacher(s) are probably best placed to gain the perceptions of parents and children. External monitoring by Ofsted will measure the effectiveness of relationships with partner institutions and families. Inspectors are asked to:

- evaluate the impact on both parents and children of any visits that are made to children and parents before children enter school;
- find out whether the induction programmes, particularly in nursery and Reception, are flexible enough to suit the needs of all children;
- evaluate the extent to which parents and toddlers and babies are encouraged to come into school, and how easy it is for parents to borrow books and other resources for children;
- examine the effectiveness of arrangements for contacts with pupils' homes, to identify and help children who are unhappy, and for involving parents who rarely come near the school.

Ofsted suggests that inspectors examine the quality of information provided for parents as part of their evaluation and examine:

- any policies on home–school contracts and the extent to which they work;
- what account the school takes of what parents know about their own child's learning;
- how far parents and teachers can talk informally together about children, and the arrangements that are made for parents whose first language is not English;
- whether reports to parents about pupils' progress tell them clearly what their children are doing, how well they are doing it, whether it is good enough and what they need to do to improve;
- to what extent written reports are followed up and discussed with parents;
- the extent to which pupils' reports and records incorporate the views of parents and show the action agreed to help pupils learn;
- how well the school helps parents to understand what is taught;

- the extent to which any home–school agreements contribute to pupils' learning;
- the extent to which parents know about and use lending libraries for toys and books;
- whether parents of children with special educational needs are properly involved in identifying their needs, provide appropriate support and regularly review their child's progress;
- how well the school communicates with parents who have disabilities, learning difficulties or who live a long way from the school without easy transport;
- how well the school consults parents about its curriculum and about major spending decisions within its application of the consultation principle in the best value framework. (Ofsted 1999b: 90)

✎ **Activity 16.1**

Use the following grid to identify aspects of monitoring transitions and transfers.

Monitoring induction: Who does what?

Head teacher	Induction coordinator/ team leader	Reception class teacher(s)	External assessor, e.g. LEA/Ofsted

Gaining children's views

> There is now increasing recognition and acceptance that children's views and perspectives need to be heard both as an ethical imperative and also as a matter of practical utility and efficacy. (Davie and Galloway 1996: 3)

Children are experts when it comes to their own lives. By listening to their views, teachers can extend their knowledge of children's perceptions of the experience and help children gain a sense of ownership for any decisions that are made regarding the induction procedures. Children's perspectives can be gained through:

- using a puppet that children can 'talk through' to tell their story of starting school;
- having a toy that children can 'help through the start of school';
- using circle time activities to ask how the start of school could be made better;
- encouraging children to draw pictures of how they felt before they started school and after the start of school.

Hebenstreit-Muller (2001) suggests the child's perspective can be ascertained through answers to the following questions:

Child to educator:
- Will you give me time to get to know myself?
- Will you protect and support me?
- Will you comfort and console me if I am sad?
- Will you like my mother/father?

Educator to child:
- Will you find 'access' to me?
- Will I understand your signals?
- Will I be able to find out what you need?
- Will you get on with the other children?
- Will you find your feet here and settle in?

Gaining parents' views

How can parents be involved in evaluating the induction? One way is by having a feedback meeting of all new parents combined with an information evening. In groups, parents could be asked to identify their perceptions of the induction process for them and their children. This could also be done through a questionnaire. Areas for consideration are:

- the documentation;
- the meetings/visits to school;
- the amount and quality of information about the induction process itself and about school;
- children's ability to settle;
- parental involvement.

✎ **Activity 16.2**

Devise a questionnaire to find out how parents viewed the induction process at your school. What helped their child to settle, what hindered? How could the school make induction better for them and their child? How could school improve the communication with parents during induction?

Gaining teachers' views

Aspects of teachers' views might include:

- the extent to which the programme has helped children in their class settle;
- the extent to which teachers were kept informed during induction;
- the amount of information that teachers gained about children's prior learning before they started school.

Team leaders can also monitor the way teachers help children settle, their sensitivity to children's emotional well-being and disposition to learn, and their ability to help children with their social skills and in becoming resilient.

Teachers may consider how they might identify signs of assimilation during the settling-in period and how they record signs of settling in (see Chapter 13) and monitor danger signs such as children:

- with high levels of crying;
- who appear disorientated;
- not joining in;
- not responding to questions;
- avoiding direct activities;
- avoiding eye contact;
- not engaging in humour;
- reluctant to engage with adults;
- who are obsessive about items of clothing;
- who are over-confident;
- who are slow within particular situations.

Evaluating induction

> Because young children do not protest in ways which no one can fail to understand, it is easy for them to become the victims of people who think it does not really matter whether they . . . have to change their teachers very often, or who will even pause to consider whether this or that form of organisation, however administratively convenient it may be . . . is really right for them. We need to be constantly asking ourselves not whether young children *can* 'take it' but whether it is the best we can do for their fullest development. (Gardner 1971: 3)

Part of the management of transitions is a consideration of the number of transitions that pupils undergo and review of the work on partnership at each transition and transfer. Having gained the information from the monitoring audit, it is necessary to use this to improve the design and policy of transition systems and reduce problems on transfer. Figure 16.1 might be useful for evaluating the induction programme and monitoring any changes that take place as a result.

All areas cannot be addressed at once so it is best to focus on one or two areas at a time. For example, looking at the sufficiency and quality of information for parents might include examining printed and oral information, statutory information in the school prospectus, timeliness and the ability to listen to parents. Another area to consider is the induction policy statement.

If children settle well in their first few months at school then it is likely that they will be successful later. The first contact with the new setting, therefore, is a crucial period as discontinuities may impact on children's acculturation to school and disrupt their learning. The stress that some children experience during transition and transfer is now recognised and many schools have implemented transition programmes that are carefully planned and well managed in order to help children make a seamless transition. Part of this involves co-ordinating the links between home, pre-transfer school and

Evaluating the induction programme						
Item	Action required	Cost and resources	Who is responsible	Success criteria	Date completed	Review date

Figure 16.1 Evaluating the induction programme

✎ Activity 16.3

The induction policy is a statement of aims and objectives of practice that reflects what happens in the setting. It should inform and guide staff. Look at the following extract from an early years policy where the nursery and school are in the same building. Consider how it might be improved.

Parents

A parent/child sheet is filled out upon entry. This allows parents to write about the positive aspects of their child. A meeting is held for new parents prior to the child beginning. They are encouraged to ask questions and voice any concerns they may have. They are also given a booklet to reinforce the information.

Links with the nursery

Most children feed through from the nursery on the premises. We have developed relationships with the staff that enable us to talk about children before they start, as well as once they have started. We hope to continue sharing outings with them.

If a child comes from another playgroup or nursery and we have concerns, we will contact them to discuss the child and request any relevant paperwork, if appropriate.

Transfer from nursery

The children in the nursery feed mainly into our school.

- The children are familiar with the main school as they:
  - attend assemblies and have large apparatus in the hall twice a week;
  - use the swimming pool in the summer and sometimes play in the infants playground, using the climbing apparatus or the field;
  - use the field for sports day;
  - use the school grounds for walks, collecting natural materials, looking at seasonal changes etc.
- The Reception teacher visits the nursery class to read a story.
- Leavers are invited to go to the Reception class for a short while. A member of staff accompanies them to help them feel secure.
- All record sheets are passed on to the Reception teacher and children are discussed. This is used to group children or pass on any particular concerns.

Is your policy available for all parents and staff to read? Does it give suggestions on how everyone can work together to help children settle? Having a policy will not in itself enable children to settle. Even if there is a policy, the time it takes for each child to settle will depend on the needs of the individual. Some children will settle more quickly than others and some may show signs of unsettled behaviour after appearing to settle in well.

schools to help children make sense of their new setting and feel in control of their lives.

Successful transitions and transfers are those where children become familiar with the environment and ways of learning in the new setting quickly and easily; where they can bring their culture to the school's culture and merge the two; where high levels of social and emotional well-being enable them to learn with confidence; and where children have high self-esteem.

Emerging from this book are some key principles for successful transitions and transfers that include:

- Schools having a transition and transfer co-ordinator who is able to take a strategic overview;
- Schools providing pre-entry visits for children and their parents that take place in a calm environment;
- Schools having systems that allow for high-quality communication between family, pre-transfer settings and school, where information is both given and received;
- Schools being sensitive to the needs of individuals and particular groups and having strategies in place to support them;
- Admission procedures that give children and their parents the opportunity to have a positive start to their first day;
- Children starting school with a friend and schools helping children to make friends;
- Schools having strategies to help children develop resilience to cope with change;
- Continuity of learning that comes about from establishing prior learning and where children are helped to learn with and from each other;
- Schools evaluating induction and the managament of transitions and transfers from the perspective of all stakeholders.

References

Alexander, T. (1996) 'Learning begins at home: implications for a learning society', in Bastiani, J. and Wolfendale, S. (eds) *Home–School Work in Britain*. London: David Fulton Publishers.

Ball, C. (1994) *Start Right: The Importance of Early Learning*. London: The Royal Society for the Encouragement of Arts, Manufactures and Commerce.

Ballinger, A. (2000) 'Psychological dimensions to transition'. Paper presented at the Wiltshire County Council Smoothing out Turbulence Conference, 6 July, Bradford-on-Avon, Bath.

Ballinger, A. (2001) 'Mobility: information for teachers and other staff who work with service children'. Paper presented at the Shropshire Service Schools' Conference: Pupil Mobility: What does it mean?/What can we do? 9 July, Albrighton.

Barbour, N. (1995) 'The development of authentic parent-centre partnerships in a child development laboratory: becoming a family centred program'. Paper presented at 5th European Early Childhood Education Research Association Conference on Quality in Early Childhood Education, Paris: 7–9 September.

Barrett, G. (1986) *Starting School: An Evaluation of the Experience*. London: Assistant Masters and Mistresses Association.

Bastiani, J. (1993) *Your Home–School Links* (revised edn.). London: New Education Press.

Bastiani, J. (1995) *Taking a Few Risks*. London: The Royal Society for the Encouragement of Arts, Manufactures and Commerce.

Bastiani, J. and Doyle, N. (1994) *Home and School: Building a Better Partnership*. London: National Consumer Council.

Bell, D. and Ritchie, R. (1999) *Towards Effective Subject Leadership in the Primary School*. Buckingham: Open University Press.

Bennet, C. and Downes, P. (1998) 'Leading parents to fuller involvement'. *Management in Education*, **12** (5), 12–14.

Bennett, N. and Kell, J. (1989) *A Good Start? Four Year Olds in Infant Schools*. Oxford: Basil Blackwell.

Bernard Van Leer Foundation (1993) 'Transition'. *Bernard Van Leer Foundation Newsletter*, **70**, 1–13.

Berrueta-Clement, J., Schweinhart, L. J., Barnett, W. S., Epstein, A. S. and Weikart, D. P. (1984) 'Changed lives: the effects of the Perry pre-school programme on youths through age 19'. *Monographs of the High/Scope Educational Research Foundation*, **8**.

Bhopal, K., Gundara, J., Jones, C. and Owen, C. (2000) 'Working towards inclusive education: aspects of good practice for gypsy traveller pupils'. *Research Brief No. 238*. London: DfEE.

Bird, M. (2001) 'Is culture just for humans?' *Time*, **158** (6), 52.

Black, P. (1998) *Testing: Friend or Foe?* London: Falmer Press.

Blatchford, P. (1999) 'The state of play in schools', in Woodhead, M., Faulkener, D. and Littleton, K. (eds) *Making Sense of Social Development*. London: Routledge, in association with The Open University.

Bleach, K. (1999) *The Induction and Mentoring of Newly Qualified Teachers: A New Deal for Teachers*. London: David Fulton Publishers.

Boyd, B. and Simpson, M. (2000) *Developing a Framework for Effective Learning and Teaching in S1/S2 in Angus Secondary Schools*. Arbroath: Angus Council Education.

Bredekamp, S. (ed.) (1987) *Developmentally Appropriate Practice in Early Childhood Programs Serving Children from Birth through Age 8*. Washington DC: National Association for the Education of Young Children.

Bronfenbrenner, U. (1979) *The Ecology of Human Development: Experiments by Nature and Design*. Massachusetts: Harvard University Press.

Brophy, J. and Statham, J. (1994) 'Measure for measure: values, quality and evaluation', in Moss, P. and Pence, A. (eds) *Valuing Quality in Early Childhood Services*. London: Paul Chapman Publishing.

Brostrom, S. (2000) 'Transition to school'. Paper presented at 10th European Early Childhood Education Research Association Conference on Quality in Early Childhood Education, University of London: 29 August – 1 September.

Brown, S. and Cleave, S. (1994) *Four Year Olds in School: Quality Matters* (2nd edn). Slough: NFER.

Bruce, T. (1996) *Helping Young Children to Play*. London: Hodder and Stoughton.

Bruce, T., Findlay, A., Read, J. and Scarborough, M. (1995) *Recurring Themes in Education*. London: Paul Chapman Publishing.

Bruner, J. S. (1996a) *The Culture of Education*. Massachusetts: Harvard University Press.

Bruner, J. S. (1996b) 'What we have learned about early learning', *European Early Childhood Education Research Journal*, **4** (1), 5–16.

Burke, P. J. (1987) *Teacher Development: Induction, Renewal and Redirection*. East Sussex: Falmer Press.

Burrell, A. and Bubb, S. (2000) 'Teacher Feedback in the Reception Class: Associations with Children's Positive Adjustment to School', *Education 3–13*, **28** (3), 58–69.

Burtscher, I. M. (1997) 'Hypotheses to explain separation problems and pedagogical advice for parents and early childhood teachers to ease children's separation from their mother when starting nursery school: a critical analysis'. Paper presented at 7th European Early Childhood Education Research Association Conference on Quality in Early Childhood Education, Munich: 3–6 September.

Campbell, C. (2000) 'Our children start school too early', *Early Years Educator*, **2** (7), 3–4.

Campbell Clark, S. (2000) 'Work/family border theory: a new theory of work/family balance', *Human Relations*, **53** (6), 747–70.

Chislett, M. (2001) 'Turbulence and Mobility'. Paper presented at the Shropshire Service Schools' Conference: Pupil Mobility: What does it mean?/ What can we do? 9 July, Albrighton.

Claxton, G. (1998) *Hare Brain Tortoise Mind*. London: Fourth Estate Limited.

Cleave, S. and Brown, S. (1989) *Four Year Olds in School: Meeting Their Needs*. Slough: National Foundation for Educational Research.

Cleave, S. and Brown, S. (1991) *Early To School: Four Year Olds in Infant Classes*. London: NFER/Routledge.

Cleave, S. and Brown, S. (1993) 'A Fair Deal for Fours', *Child Education*, **70** (4), 23–6.

Cleave, S., Jowett, S. and Bate, M. (1982) . . . *And So To School: A Study of Continuity from Pre-school to Infant School*. Berkshire: NFER-Nelson.

Cohen, A. (1988) *Early Education: The Parents' Role*. London: Paul Chapman Publishing.

Corsaro, W. A. (1981) 'Friendship in the Nursery School: Social Organization in a Peer Environment', in Asher, S. R. and Gottman, J. M. (eds) *The Development of Children's Friendships*. Cambridge: Cambridge University Press.

Cousins, J. (1990) 'Are your little Humpty Dumpties floating or sinking? What sense do children of four make of reception class at school? Different conceptions at the time of transition', *Early Years*, **10** (2), 28–38.

Cousins, J. (1999) 'It Takes Time', *Nursery World*, **99** (3665), 10–11.

Crosser, S. L. (1991) 'Summer birth date children: kindergarten entrance age and academic achievement', *Journal of Educational Research*, **84** (3), 140–6.

Curtis, A. M. (1986) *A Curriculum for the Pre-school Child*. London: NFER-Nelson.

Dahlberg, G. and Asen, G. (1994) 'Evaluation and Regulation: A Question of Empowerment', in Moss, P. and Pence, A. (eds) *Valuing Quality in Early Childhood Services*. London: Paul Chapman Publishing.

Dahlberg, G., Moss, P. and Pence, A. (1999) *Beyond Quality in Early Childhood Education and Care: Postmodern Perspectives.* London: Falmer Press.

Dalli, C. (1999) 'Learning to Be in Childcare: Mothers' Stories of their Child's "Settling-in"', *European Early Childhood Education Research Journal,* **7** (2), 53–66.

David, T. (1990) *Under Five – Under Educated?* Milton Keynes: Open University Press.

Davie, R. and Galloway, D. (1996) 'The Voice of the Child in Education', in Davie, R. and Galloway, D. (eds) *Listening to Children in Education.* London: David Fulton Publishers.

Day, J. (1995) 'Stepping Out Together', *Children UK,* **5**, 12–13.

Deegan, J. G. (1996) *Children's Friendships in Culturally Diverse Classrooms.* London: Falmer Press.

Department for Education (1994) *Our Children's Education: The Updated Parent's Charter.* London: HMSO.

Department for Education and Employment (1997a) 'Checklist for private, voluntary and independent providers', *News Sheet: Nursery Education News.* August. London: Department for Education and Employment.

Department for Education and Employment (1997b) *Excellence in Schools (White Paper).* London: The Stationery Office.

Department for Education and Employment (1998) *Home–School Agreements. Guidance for Schools.* Sudbury, Suffolk: DfEE Publications.

Department of Education and Science (1967) *Children and Their Primary Schools.* A Report by the Central Advisory Council for Education, chaired by Lady Plowden. London: HMSO.

Department of Education and Science (1990) *Starting with Quality.* The Report of the Committee of Inquiry into the Quality of the Educational Experience Offered to Three- and Four-year-olds, chaired by Angela Rumbold. London: HMSO.

Department of Education and Science (1991) *Circular No. 6/91: Implementation of More Open Enrolment in Primary Schools.* London: HMSO.

Department of Education and Science/Welsh Office (1977) *A New Partnership for Our Schools* (The Taylor Report). London: HMSO.

Department of Education Northern Ireland (2000) 'From Pre-school to School: A Review of the Research Literature', *Research Briefing 3/2000.* Statistics and Research Agency and Department of Education.

Dobson, J. (2000) 'Pupil Mobility: What, Where and Why?' Paper presented at the Wiltshire County Council Smoothing out Turbulence Conference, 6 July, Bradford-on-Avon, Bath.

Dowling, M. (1988) *Education 3 to 5: A Teachers' Handbook.* London: Paul Chapman Publishing.

Dowling, M. (1995) *Starting School at Four: A Joint Endeavour*. London: Paul Chapman Publishing.

Dowling, M. (2000) *Young Children's Personal, Social and Emotional Development*. London: Paul Chapman Publishing.

Dunlop, A. W. A. (2001) 'Children's Thinking about Transitions to School'. Paper presented at 11th European Early Childhood Education Research Association Conference on Quality in Early Childhood Education. Alkmaar, The Netherlands, 29 August – 1 September.

Edwards, A. and Knight, P. (1994) *Effective Early Years Education*. Buckingham: Open University Press.

Elfer, P. (1997) 'Emotional Literacy in the Nursery', *Children UK*, **15**, 14.

Elkin, S. (1998) 'The Risky Game of Classroom Musical Chairs', *The Sunday Times*, 20 September, 29.

Emery, H. (1993) 'Baseline Assessment: A National Survey', *Child Education*, **70** (9), 7–10.

European Commission: Education and Care (2000) *Key Data on Education in Europe 1999–2000*. Luxembourg: Office for Official Publications of the European Communities.

Everard, B. and Morris, G. (1996) *Effective School Management* (3rd edn). London: Paul Chapman Publishers.

Fabian, H. (1996) 'Children Starting School: Parents in Partnership', *Mentoring and Tutoring*, **4** (1), 12–22.

Fabian, H. (1998) *'Induction to School and Transitions through Key Stage One: Practice and Perceptions'*. Unpublished PhD thesis.

Fabian, H. (2000) 'Small Steps to Starting School', *International Journal of Early Years Education*, **8** (2), 141–53.

Fieldhouse, J. (1988) 'Going to School', *Management in Education*, **2** (4), 28–9.

Fonagy, P., Steele, M., Steele, H., Higgit, A. and Target, M. (1994) 'The theory and practice of resilience', *Journal of Child Psychology and Psychiatry*, **35** (2), 231–57.

Foskett, N. H. (1998) 'Schools and Marketization: Cultural Challenges and Responses', *Educational Management and Administration*, **26** (2), 197–210.

Fthenakis, W. E. and Textor, M. R. (1998) *Qualitat von Kinderbetreuung: deutsche und internationale perspektiven*. Weinheim und Basel: Beltz, in Fthenakis, W. E. (1998) 'Family Transitions and Quality in Early Childhood Education', *European Early Childhood Education Research Journal*, **6** (1), 5–17.

Galton, M., Gray, J. and Rudduck, J. (1999a) *The Impact of School Transitions and Transfers on Pupil Progress and Attainment: Research Report RR131*. London: DfEE, HMSO.

Galton, M., Gray, J. and Rudduck, J. (1999b) 'The Impact of School Transitions and Transfers on Pupil Progress and Attainment', *Research Brief No. 131*. London: DfEE.

Gardner, D. E. M. (1971) 'Looking at Children Now – Young Children', *Froebel Journal*, **20**, 3–8.

Gewirtz, S., Ball, S. J. and Bowe, R. (1995) *Markets, Choice and Equity in Education*. Milton Keynes: Open University Press.

Ghaye, A. and Pascal, C. (1988) 'Four-year-old children in reception classrooms: participant perceptions and practice', *Educational Studies*, **14** (2), 187–208.

Gipps, C., McCallum, B. and Brown, M. (1996) 'Models of teacher assessment among primary school teachers in England', *The Curriculum Journal*, **2** (7), 167–83.

Goleman, D. (1996) *Emotional Intelligence*. London: Bloomsbury Publishing.

Goleman, D. (1998) *Working with Emotional Intelligence*. London: Bloomsbury Publishing.

Gregory, E. and Biarnes, J. (1994) 'Tony and Jean-Francois Looking for Sense in the Strangeness of School', in Dombey, H. and Meek Spencer, M. (eds) *First Steps Together*. Stoke-on-Trent: Trentham Books.

Griebel, W. and Niesel, R. (1997) 'From Family to Kindergarten: A Common Experience in a Transition Perspective'. Paper presented at 7th European Early Childhood Education Research Association Conference on Quality in Early Childhood Education, Munich: 3–6 September.

Griebel, W. and Niesel, R. (1999) 'From Kindergarten to School: A Transition for the Family'. Paper presented at 9th European Early Childhood Education Research Association Conference on Quality in Early Childhood Education, Helsinki: 1–4 September.

Griebel, W. and Niesel, R. (2000) 'The children's voice in the complex transition into kindergarten and school'. Paper presented at 10th European Early Childhood Education Research Association Conference on Quality in Early Childhood Education, London: 29 August – 1 September.

Gura, P. (1996) 'Roles and Relationships', in Robson, S. and Smedley, S. (eds) *Education in Early Childhood*. London: David Fulton Publishers.

Hallgarten, J. (2000) 'Involving the parents: parent–school relationships', *Education Journal*, **50**, 10–11.

Hannon, P., and James, S. (1990) 'Parents' and Teachers' Perspectives on Preschool Literacy Development', *British Educational Research Journal*, **16** (3), 259–72.

Harkness, S. and Super, C. M. (1994) 'Parental Ethnotheories in Culture and Human Development', *Researching Early Childhood*, **2** (1), 59–84.

Hartup, W. W. (1991) 'Having Friends, Making Friends, and Keeping Friends: Relationships as Educational Contexts', *ERIC Digest*. Champaign: University of Illinois.

Hay, S. (1997) *Essential Nursery Management*. London: Bailliere Tindall.

Hebenstreit-Muller, S. (2001) 'How do we establish respect for individuality and children's views as a quality standard for kindergartens?' Paper presented at 11th European Early Childhood Education Research Association Conference on Quality in Early Childhood Education, Alkmaar, The Netherlands: 29 August – 1 September.

Hennessy, E. (1998) 'My First Teacher', *Nursery World*, **98** (3625), 14–15.

Holliday, B. (2001) 'Is school always the best way to start?', *Early Years Educator*, **2** (9), 6–7.

House of Commons (2001) *Government's Response to the First Report from the Committee Session 2000–2001: Early Years.* London: The Stationery Office.

Hubberstey, S. (1994) 'Do Your Homework First!' *Big School.* Nursery World Publications, 4–5.

Hughes, M., Pinkerton, G. and Plewis, I. (1979) 'Children's Difficulties on Starting Infant School', *Journal of Child Psychology and Psychiatry*, **20**, 187–96.

Hughes, M., Wikeley, F. and Nash, T. (1994) *Parents and their Children's Schools.* Oxford: Blackwell Publishers.

Huttunen, E. 'Children's experiences in early childhood programmes', *International Journal of Early Childhood*, **24**, 3–11.

Illsley Clarke, J. (1997) 'Self Esteem and the Family', *The Self Esteem Directory.* Kent: Smallwood Publishing.

James, A. and Prout, A. (1997) 'Re-Presenting Childhood: Time and Transition in the Study of Childhood', in James, A. and Prout, A. (eds) *Constructing and Reconstructing Childhood: Contemporary Issues in the Sociological Study of Childhood* (2nd edn). London: Falmer Press.

Jordan, E. (2000) 'Traveller Pupils and Scottish Schools', *Spotlights*, **76**, Edinburgh: The Scottish Council for Research in Education.

Kell, C. (1992) 'Rites of Passage', *The Times Educational Supplement.* October 23, A8.

Kienig, A. (1997) 'The Child Enters Pre-school Setting'. Poster presented at 7th European Early Childhood Education Research Association Conference on Quality in Early Childhood Education, Munich: 3–6 September.

Kienig, A. (1998) 'Transitions in Early Childhood'. Paper presented at 8th European Early Childhood Education Research Association Conference on Quality in Early Childhood Education, Santiago di Compostella, Spain: 2–5 September.

Klein, R. (1993) 'In Search of the Super-ego', *The Times Educational Supplement.* September.

Krovetz, M. L. (1999) *Fostering Resiliency.* California: Corwin Press.

Kurtz-Costes, B., McCall, R. and Schneider, W. (1997) 'Implications from Developmental Cross-cultural Research for the Study of Acculturation in Western Civilisations', in Tudge, J., Shanahan, M. J. and Valsiner, J. (eds) *Comparisons in Human Development: Understanding Time and Context.* Cambridge: Cambridge University Press.

Laevers, F., Vandenbussche, E., Kog, M. and Depondt, L. (1997) *A Process-oriented Child Monitoring System for Young Children*. Centre for Experiential Education: Katholieke Universiteit Leuven.

Langsted, O. (1994) 'Looking at quality from the child's perspective', in Moss, P. and Pence, A. (eds) *Valuing Quality in Early Childhood Services*. London: Paul Chapman Publishers.

Lawrence, I. (1994) 'After 1994: Where Are we Going?', in Lawrence, I. (ed.) *Education Tomorrow*. London: Cassell.

Lombardi, J. (1992) Beyond Transition: Ensuring Continuity in Early Childhood Services. *ERIC Digest*. Champaign: University of Illinois.

Long, R. (2000) 'Schooling for the information society', *Management in Education*, **14** (3), 25.

Long, R. (2001) 'Stress-Proofing the Pupils', *Five to Seven*, **1** (3), 38–40.

Maclachlan, K. (1995) 'Encouraging the Clients – Parents and Young Children', *Management in Education*, **9** (1), 6–7.

Madge, N. (2001) 'Supporting Children Through Transition', *Children Now*, **8**, 12.

Mansfield, M. (1999) 'Home–school agreements', *CEDC* 6.

Margetts, K (2000) 'Transition to School – Complexity and Diversity'. Paper presented at 10th European Early Childhood Education Research Association Conference on Quality in Early Childhood Education, London: 29 August – 1 September.

Marshall, P. (1988) *Transition and Continuity in the Educational Process*. London: Kogan Page.

McGavin, H. (2001) 'Room with a Hue', *The Times Educational Supplement*, 2 February, 14–15.

McPake, J. and Powney, J. (1998) 'A mirror to ourselves? The educational experiences of Japanese children at school in the UK', *Educational Research*, **40** (2), 169–79.

Meighan, R. (1997) *The Next Learning System: and why home-schoolers are trailblazers*. Nottinghamshire: Educational Heretics Press.

Meighan, R. and Siraj-Blatchford, I. (1997) *A Sociology of Educating* (3rd edn). London: Cassell.

Miller, S. (1994) 'Parent Potential', *Child Education*, **71** (1), 52–3.

Morrison, I. (2000) '"School's great – apart from the lessons": Sustaining the excitement of learning post-transfer', *Improving Schools*, **3** (1), 46–9.

Moss, P. (2000) 'Foreign Services', *Nursery World*, **100** (3733) 10–14.

Moss, P. (2001) 'True joined-up thinking', *Nursery World*, **101** (3765), 34.

Moss, P. and Pence, A. (eds) (1994) *Valuing Quality in Early Childhood Services*. London: Paul Chapman Publishers.

National Curriculum Council (1989) *A Framework for the Primary Curriculum*. London: NCC.

National Foundation for Educational Research/School Curriculum Development Committee (1987) *Four-Year-Olds in School: Policy and Practice*. NFER/SCDC.

Neisser, U. (1993) 'The Self Perceived', in Neisser, U. (ed.) *The Perceived Self: Ecological and Interpersonal Sources of Self-knowledge*. Cambridge University Press.

Neuman, M. (2000) 'Hand in Hand: Improving the links between ECEC and schools in OECD countries'. Paper prepared for the Consultative Committee on International Developments in ECEC: The Institute for Child and Family Policy, Columbia University: May 11–12.

Neville, M. (1995) 'Social Culture and Effectiveness in an Asian Pluralistic Society', *International Studies in Educational Administration*, **23** (2), 28–37.

Nutbrown, C. (1994) *Threads of Thinking*. London: Paul Chapman Publishing.

Nutbrown, C. (ed.) (1996) *Respectful Educators – Capable Learners: Children's Rights and Early Education*. London: Paul Chapman Publishing.

Office for Standards in Education (1995) *Guidance on the Inspection of Nursery and Primary Schools*. London: HMSO.

Office for Standards in Education (1998) *Guidance on the Inspection of Nursery Education Provision in the Private, Voluntary and Independent Sectors*. London: The Stationery Office.

Office for Standards in Education (1999) *Raising the Attainment of Minority Ethnic Pupils: School and LEA responses*. London: Ofsted.

Office for Standards in Education (1999a) *School Inspection: A Guide to the Law: September 1999*. London: Ofsted.

Office for Standards in Education. (1999b) *Handbook for Inspecting Primary and Nursery Schools*. London: The Stationery Office.

Office for Standards in Education (2000) *Inspecting Subjects 3–11: Guidance for Inspectors in Schools*. London: Ofsted.

Osgood, J. and Sharp, C. (2000) *Developing Early Education and Childcare Services for the 21st Century*. Slough: The National Foundation for Educational Research.

Ouston, J. and Hood, S. (2000) *Home–School Agreements: A True Partnership?* London: The Research and Information on State Education Trust (RISE).

Parker-Jenkins, M., Briggs, D., Taylor-Basil, V., Hartas, D., Brook, D., Claridge, B., Hewitt, D., Hewson, J., Leyand, G., Kay, J., Taylor, V., Tresadern, J., Wakefield, P., Wakefield, C., Warren, C. and Zelnskyj, J. (2001) 'One Year On: the implementation and impact of the Home–School Agreements in Derbyshire primary schools', *Management in Education*, **15** (1), 29–32.

Pascal, C. (1990) *Under-Fives in the Infant Classroom*. Stoke-on-Trent: Trentham Books.

Pedersen, E., Faucher, T. A. and Eaton, W. W. (1978) 'A New Perspective on the

Effects of First-grade Teachers on Children's Subsequent Adult Status', *Harvard Educational Review*, **48**, 1–31.

Pianta, R. C., Cox, M. J., Taylor, L. and Early, D. (1999) 'Kindergarten Teachers' Practices Related to the Transition to School: Results of a National Survey', *The Elementary School Journal*, **100** (1), 71–86, in Brostrom, S. (2000) 'Transition to school'. Paper presented at 10th European Early Childhood Education Research Association Conference on Quality in Early Childhood Education, University of London: 29 August – 1 September.

Pollard, A. (1996) *The Social World of Children's Learning*. London: Cassell.

Pollock, D. and Van Reken, R. (1999) *Third Culture Kids: Growing Up Among Worlds*. Yarmouth, ME: Intercultural Press.

Prais, S. J. (1997) 'School Readiness, Whole-class Teaching and Pupils' Mathematical Attainment', *Discussion Paper 111*. London: National Institute of Economic and Social Research.

Pramling Samuelsson, I., Johansson, E., Davidsson, B. and Fors, B. (2000) 'Student Teachers' and Preschool Children's Questions about Life – A Phenomenographic Approach to Learning', *European Early Childhood Education Research Journal*, **8** (2), 5–22.

Pugh, G. (1996) 'Four-year-olds in school: What is appropriate provision?' *Children UK*. Winter Issue 11.

Pugh, G., De'Ath, E. and Smith, C. (1994) *Confident Parents, Confident Children: Policy and Practice in Parent Education and Support*. London: National Children's Bureau.

Putallaz, M. and Gottman, J. M. (1981) 'Social Skills and Group Acceptance', in Asher, S. R. and Gottman, J. M. (eds) *The Development of Children's Friendships*. Cambridge: Cambridge University Press.

Qualifications and Curriculum Authority (1998) *The Baseline Assessment Information Pack*. London: QCA Publications.

Qualifications and Curriculum Authority (1999) *Early Learning Goals*. London: QCA.

Qualifications and Curriculum Authority (2000) *Curriculum Guidance for the Foundation Stage*. London: QCA.

Read, K. and Patterson, J. (1976) *The Nursery School and Kindergarten: Human Relationships and Learning* (7th edn). New York: Holt, Rinehart and Winston.

Robson, S. (1996) 'Home and School: A Potentially Powerful Partnership', in Robson, S. and Smedley, S. (eds) *Education in Early Childhood*. London: David Fulton Publishers.

Rogers, C. (1983) *Freedom to Learn for the Eighties*. USA: McMillan Merrill.

Rudduck, J. (1996) 'Going to "the big school": the turbulence of transition', in Rudduck, J., Chaplain, R. and Wallace, G. (eds) *School Improvement: What Can Pupils Tell us?* London: David Fulton Publishers.

Rutter, M. (1997) 'Psychosocial Adversity: Risk, Resilience and Recovery'. Keynote Lecture given at 7th European Early Childhood Education Research Association Conference on Quality in Early Childhood Education, Munich: 3–6 September.

Rutter, M. and Rutter, M. (1992) *Developing Minds: Challenge and Continuity across the Life Span*. London: Penguin.

School Curriculum and Assessment Authority (1996) *Nursery Education: Desirable Outcomes for Children's Learning on Entering Compulsory Education*. London: DfEE and SCAA.

School Curriculum and Assessment Authority (1997) *The National Framework for Baseline Assessment*. London: SCAA.

Sharp, C. (1995) *School Entry and the Impact of Season of Birth on Attainment*. Slough: NFER Research Summary.

Sharp, C. (1998) 'Age of Starting School and the Early Years Curriculum'. Paper presented at the NFER Annual Conference, London: 6 October.

Sharp, P. (2001) *Nurturing Emotional Literacy*. London: David Fulton Publishers.

Sherman, A. (1996) *Rules, Routines and Regimentation*. Nottingham: Educational Heretics Press.

Smith, T. (1980) *Parents and Preschool*. Oxford Research Project. London: Grant McIntyre.

Stead, J., Closs, A. and Arshad, R. (1999) 'Refugee Pupils in Scottish Schools', *Spotlights 74*. Edinburgh: The Scottish Council for Research in Education.

Stelling, C. and Fabian, H. (1996) 'An Open Door', *Child Education*, **73** (1), 54–5.

Stevens, L. (1998) 'Transitions'. Paper presented at Child Guidance Conference, Lubbeke, Germany.

Stevenson, C. (1988) *Focus on Four*. Stevenage: Area Advisory Centre.

Sylva, K. and Moss, P. (1992) 'Learning Before School', *National Commission on Education Briefing No. 8*.

Tabors, P. (1997) *One Child, Two Languages: A Guide for Pre-school Educators of Children Learning English as a Second Language*. Baltimore, MD: Paul Brookes Publishing Company.

Tharp, R. and Gallimore, R. (1998) 'A Theory of Teaching as Assisted Performance', in Faulkener, D., Littleton, K. and Woodhead, M. (eds) *Learning Relationships in the Classroom*. London: Routledge in association with The Open University.

Thyssen, S. (1997) 'The child's beginning in day care'. Paper presented at 7th European Early Childhood Education Research Association Conference on Quality in Early Childhood Education, Munich: 3–6 September.

Tizard, B. and Hughes, M. (1984) *Young Children Learning*. London: Fontana.

Tizard, B., Blatchford, P., Burke, J., Farquhar, C. and Plewis, I. (1988) *Young Children at School in the Inner City*. Hove and London: Lawrence Erlbaum Associates.

Tomlinson, H. (1993) *Croner's Head Teacher's Bulletin: Marketing the School*. Issue 2. London: Croner Publications Ltd.

Trevarthen, C. (1996) 'How a Young Child Investigates People and Things: Why Play Helps Development'. Paper presented at The TACTYC National Conference: A Celebration of Play, University of Greenwich, London: November 8–9.

Tudge, J., Gray, J. T. and Hogan, D. M. (1997) 'Ecological Perspectives in Human Development: A Comparison of Gibson and Bronfenbrenner', in Tudge, J., Shanahan, M. J. and Valsiner, J. (eds) *Comparisons in Human Development: Understanding Time and Context*. Cambridge: Cambridge University Press.

Turner, V. W. (1969) *The Ritual Process: Structure and Anti-Structure*. London: Routledge and Kegan Paul.

Van Gennep, A. (1960) *Rites of Passage* (Translation by Vizedom, M. B. and Caffee, G. L.). London: Routledge and Kegan Paul.

Vandenbussche, E., Kog, M., Depondt, L. and Laevers, F. (1994) *A Process-oriented child follow-up system for young children*. Pre-publication: Centre for Experiential Education, Katholieke Universiteit Leuven.

Vopat, J. (1994) *The Parent Project*. Maine: Stenhouse Publishers.

Vygotsky, L. S. (1978) *Mind in Society: The Development of Higher Psychological Processes* (Translated and Edited by Cole, M., John-Stiener, V., Scribner, S. and Souberman, E.). Massachusetts: Harvard University Press.

Waksler, F. C. (1996) *The Little Trials of Childhood and Children's Strategies for Dealing with Them*. London: Falmer Press.

Waterland, L. (1994) *Not a Perfect Offering: A New School Year*. Gloucester: The Thimble Press.

Wells, G. (1986) *The Meaning Makers*. London: Hodder and Stoughton.

Whitehead, M. (1998) 'The Poaching Game', *Guardian Education*, Tuesday 24 February, 2.

Willes, M. J. (1983) *Children Into Pupils*. London: Routledge and Kegan Paul.

Williams, S. (1998) 'Born too Late', *Nursery World*, **98** (3596), 10–11.

Wiltsher, A. (2000) 'A Question of Age', *Nursery World*, **100** (3711), 10–11.

Winnicott, D. W. (1974) *Playing and Reality*. Harmondsworth: Penguin Books.

Winterhoff, P. A. (1997) 'Sociocultural Promotions Constraining Children's Social Activity: Comparisons and Variability in the Development of Friendships', in Tudge, J., Shanahan, M. J. and Valsiner, J. (eds) *Comparisons in Human Development: Understanding Time and Context*. Cambridge: Cambridge University Press.

Wolfendale, S. (1989) (ed.) *Parental Involvement, Developing Networks between School, Home and Community*. London: Cassell Educational Ltd.

Woodhead, M. (1989) '"School starts at five . . . or four years old?" The rationale for changing admission policies in England and Wales', *Journal of Education Policy*, **4** (1), 1–21.

Woolfson, R. (1993) 'From Nursery to Infant Class', *Nursery World*, **93** (3369), 12–13.

Woolfson, R. (1999) 'Be Prepared', *Nursery World*, **99** (3662), 14–15.

Zill, N., Loomis, L. S. and West, J. (1997) *National Household Education Survey. The Elementary School Performance and Adjustment of Children who Enter Kindergarten Late or Repeat Kindergarten: Findings from National Surveys* (NCES Statistical Analysis Report 98–097). Washington DC: US Department of Education, National Centre for Education Statistics, in Sharp, C. (1998) 'Age of Starting School and the Early Years Curriculum'. Paper presented at the NFER Annual Conference, London: 6 October.

Name Index

Subject Index